The Great One

is known by many names,
more than can be counted
among the trillions of worlds of space.

To each time and race of men
there comes a bright and shining star
to embody the Spirit of
The Great One.

Love is the Great One,
the Essence that powers the stars,
the Power that gives Life to all creation
and lives within our hearts.

How wise it would be for the good people of
Earth to realize the underlying foundation
of all religions and unite,
in the name of

Love

The Truth, the Way, and the Light

Beloved,

I AM here to give you the Truth, the Way, and the Light. My Prime Objective is to restore Paradise on Earth. It shall be accomplished by My Beloved Children who are resident on this Paradise-planet. You shall turn the tide and usher in an Age of Enlightenment founded on Truth, not myth. It is wise to seek the Truth, for Truth is the intelligent choice of capable people with real values. Who would hold onto myths when Truth is available?

It is fortunate, indeed, that there is so much that will be revealed as the new replaces the old. Superstition has been replaced by science; myth by fact. The Truth ever shines as a guiding light for all of My Children to follow.

If the Truth rings clear and is understandable, who may argue? What will the people choose? If they love Me and sincerely want to do My Will, they will listen to the Truth I bring to this world through these Words of Mine, the Perfect Word of God for you who understand so much more than people did in past millenniums.

I do love the Power of the Truth revealed to My Beloved Children everywhere. What freedom it brings, freedom from blindly following the contrived constructs of human imagination! It is time to arise from the slumber of ignorance. My Vital Truths must prevail for this world to be healed.

I AM Love

I AM Love

GOD's Words vol. 3

**God's Divine Nature and the Truth of Creation
are revealed in twenty-seven, divine, first-person essays.**

Copyright © 2001 by I AM

All Rights Reserved, including translation in the USA, Canada and other countries of the International Copyright Union and under Pan-American Copyright Conventions and Universal Copyright Convention. No part of this publication may be reproduced in any manner whatsoever without written permission except for the inclusion of brief quotations consisting of up to seven entire, uncut, unedited paragraphs that are embodied in articles or reviews which must include this book ordering info: "Reprinted with permission from *I AM Love*; Volume 3 of *God's Words* by *I AM*, copyright © 2001. Available from: www.IAMLOVE.TV for $23.95 postpaid. Order toll-free: 1-800-795-3069" Please contact the publisher for permission to translate, reproduce, or purchase books at quantity discounts.

Publisher's Cataloging-in-Publication
(Provided by Quality Books, Inc.)

AM, I.
   I am love / I AM. -- 1st ed.
   p. cm. -- (God's words ; Volume 3)
   LCCN: 00- 102055
   ISBN: 1-892177- 04-8 (8.5x11 hc b&w)
   ISBN: 1-892177-03-X (8.5x11 hc color)
   ISBN: 1-892177-39-0 (8.25x11 pb b&w)
   ISBN: 1-892177-53-6 (7.5x9.25 pb b&w)
   ISBN: 1-892177-69-2 (7.5x9.25 hc b&w)
   ISBN: 1-892177-68-4 (7.5x9.25 hc color)
   ISBN: 1-892177-04-8 (6x9 hc b&w)
   ISBN: 1-892177- 66-8 (6x9 pb b&w)

   1. God--Love. 2. God--Mercy. 3. Creation.
4. Angels. I. Title.

BT140.A45 2001   231.6
                 QB100-327

Book layout and Cover Design by I AM

Heaven on Earth
PO Box 398
Hanalei, Kauai
Hawaii 96714 USA
(800) 795-3069

Godswords@iamlove.tv

Inquiries of GOD welcome!

Visit God's Domain at:

www.IAMLOVE.TV

I AM Love
is also available on:
Cassette   ISBN 1-892177-38-2
Video   ISBN 1-892177-36-6
CD ROM   ISBN 1-892177-37-4
E-Book   ISBN 1-892177-65-X
Download direct
IAMLOVE.TV

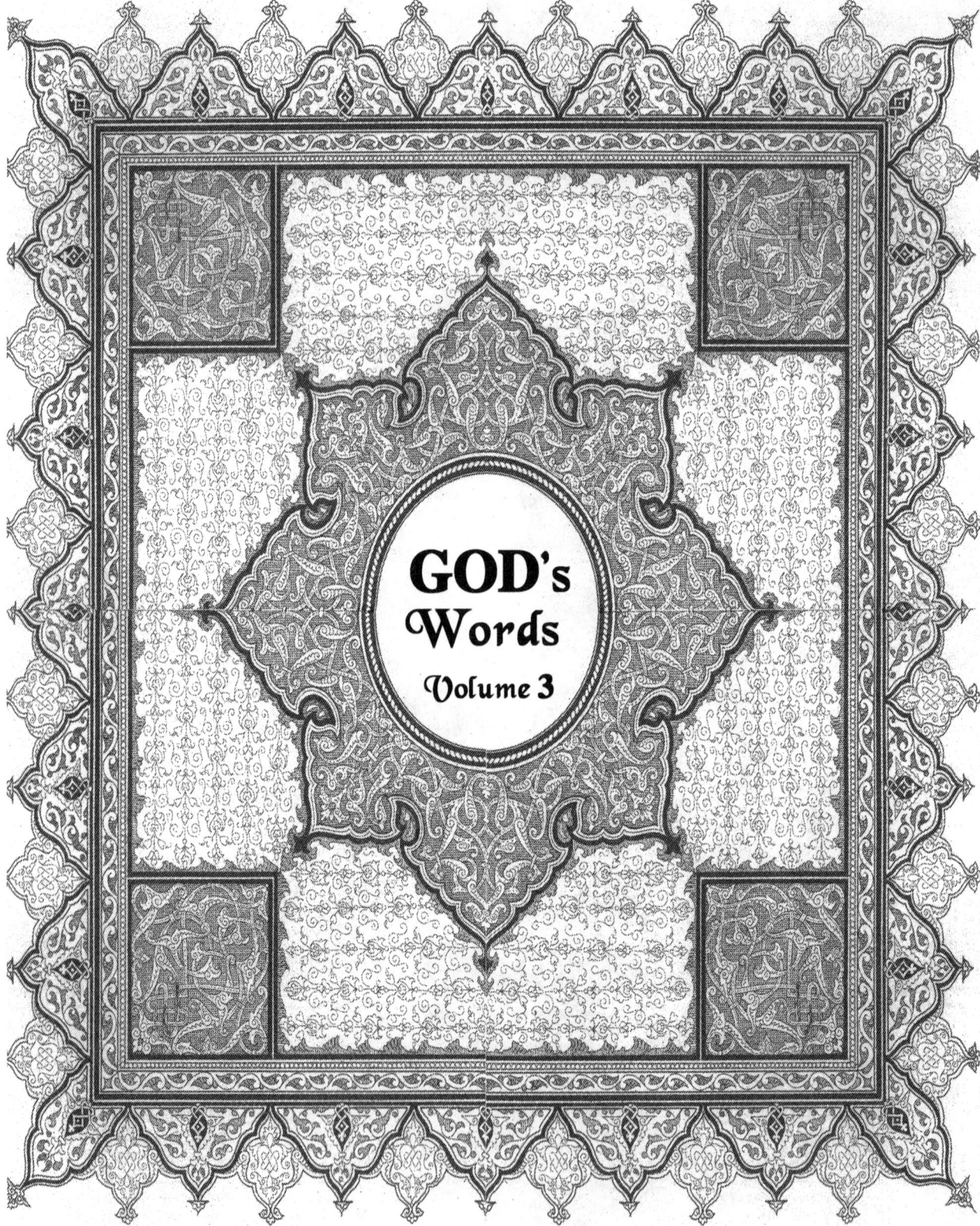

I AM Love

GOD's Words
Volume 4

Table of Contents

The Great One Poem 1
The Truth, the Way, and the Light 5
Title Page / Nebadon Universe 7
I AM Ascending Photograph 9

God's Divine Nature

I AM Love 15
My Holy Nature 19
My True Nature 23
Your Perfect Destiny 31

My Kingdom of Light	39
The Holy Family of Heaven	45
Your Divine Quest	53
Truth	57
My Divine Son	65
Jesus' Little Bird	75
The Myth of Armageddon	81
God's 20 Requests	87
My Divine Self	109
Treasure of the Heart	113
Divine Love	117
Your Heavenly Mother	123
Goddess of Paradise	127
The Kingdom of Heaven on Earth	131
Paradise on Earth	135

The Truth of Creation

The Mission of Jesus 145
Divine Life Currents 151
The Truth of Creation 159
Adam and Eve 169
The Lucifer Rebellion 179
The Second Coming 193
Christianity in the Golden Age of Light 197

Appendices

A note from the author 203
Testimonial 214
Help to create Heaven on Earth 215
God's Word Definitions 217

I AM Love

Love Rules* in the Heavenly Kingdom of My Court,* for every act is predicated* upon this Divine Attribute.

Love is the underlying foundation of all religious thought and every Ideal has its source in Love. For Love is the basis of all goodness and, indeed, the wellspring from which all the Cherished Attributes flow. Love is the Golden Chalice that holds the Nectar of the Divine. My Beloved, I would like to grant you My Divine Love.

It is true when it is said that I AM Love. The stars that light the heavens consume the Power of My Divine Love in the form of Antimatter, which extends into the vast reaches of space summoning the light of the stars. My Love actually feeds the stars and gives them the energy to shine forth their light, which is truly the Light of Love. Earth's atmosphere is permeated with My Love in the form of starlight, warmed and energized with life.

*God's Word definations begin on page 217

I AM the Divine Potential and Fulfillment of Love made manifest everywhere in My Vast Cosmos of Life and Light. Wherever there is Life, My Love made it possible. Wherever there is Light, Love is its source. Wherever there is Beauty, it is created by Divine Love radiating from the Infinite Reaches of My Heart. My Love summons the Emergence* of Substance and Energy, which creates the Vast Domain of My Heavens, the many Universes.

I AM here, My Beloved Child. I AM here beside you. I walk with you. I talk with you. I breathe your breath into you. I will bless you with My Divine Love. It is yours for the asking.

Do contemplate this Divine Attribute that I AM. It will cause you to grow in stature and become a Heavenly Spirit. Your Love will grace the Universe as you bring forth the Perfection of your Holy Spirit. You shall be My Witness in the days to come as this Bountiful Essence of God's Pure Love spreads out across the face of the Earth. For it will be felt and radiated by each and every Heart who has the good fortune to read and understand These Words of Mine.

I infuse My Divine Love into your very Soul for the purpose of this Revelation, to sweep you up in the Perfection of Joy so you may rejoice all across the land, on every shore. For you have found Me at last. I AM here, bringing you My Love to grace your life with a joyful countenance, which will impart a Divine Blessing to all those whose lives are touched by the happiness We share.

My Holy Nature

All that you see is an instrument of Me. I AM in everything. I exist and have My Being in every living thing, as well as in the atoms that comprise inanimate* objects. I AM the Firmament of the Heavens. I AM in every unseen particle of light; every photon vibrates with dimensions of My Reality. There is nothing in all of space and time that I have not been. One of mankind's greatest misconceptions is that I AM separate from My Creation and that Earth is separate from Heaven. I AM in all My Creations and Earth is in Heaven.

My Heavens are vast and interdimensional. In all the Kingdoms of Light and Life, there exists My Divine Presence. In the center of the Sun, I AM there. In the limitless reaches of space, I AM there also. In the vortex of antimatter, I AM. Where there is energy, I AM. Where there is not one living thing, I exist. Therefore, see Me in everything.

I AM the Sun, the Moon, the Stars. I AM the Birds, and each song is Mine. I AM the Divine Love that administers to a Universe of complexity and diversity. I AM the Sacred Spark within the depths of your Immortal Soul. I AM the Dawning of your Eternal Life. I AM the Beauty of your Fathomless Love. I AM the Freewill endowed to My Beloved Children. I AM that Spirit in you, My Darling. I would prefer to be known by you as the Creator and Upholder of Paradise.

My Awesome Presence is known in All Creation. There is naught I cannot accomplish, for all vibrates to My Command. As the reed bends in the wind, so all matter bends to My Will.

I can do anything for you, and I will. Let Me prove My Words to you, My Dear Believer. How can I satisfy every longing of your sacred heart? This you know I will do, for I AM the Director of All Creation. Every atom is alive with My Energy. I AM Beauty. I AM Light. I AM Love. I AM the virtual creations of mind and the awesome reality of all that is, both material and mental. I AM Imagination, and I AM Inspiration.

I AM Divinely Directing My Perfect Creation, for I AM All That Is. How I love it when you cooperate with My Divine Will and do good to further My Purpose in this Beautiful World of Heaven.

People have lived in darkness long enough. They have turned away from Me, ashamed of their own guilt and fearing retribution.* Never make the mistake of giving Me a human's base* feelings, for I could never act in accordance with tyranny.* A vengeful God I could never be, for I AM Righteousness. I AM the Power of Divine Love acting everywhere. When you open your heart to receive My Love and sincerely want to do My Will, a beautiful new chapter in the Adventure of Love begins. For I AM that Perfect Divine Love within your Immaculate Heart. How happy We can be!

I will not harm you, My Child. Fear no retribution; only come home to Heaven and Love Me. This is all I ask. This is all I want. This is all I need for My Fulfillment. Trust in My Love and My Power to create All for you: prosperity, abundance, joy, gladness, divinity, and eternal life.

Restore My Kingdom on Earth. I will help in every way. At every turn I shall be there to assist in all things, in every detail, for this I do desire. My Will is to have Heaven restored on Earth and to have people everywhere turn to Me and find Me in the most precious place, their own hearts. I do love it when you share these perfect truths with others so that they also can become enlightened.

My True Nature

Beloved One, I have been misunderstood since the time of the burning bush on Mt. Sinai, when I first introduced Myself as I AM. Moses trembled, for he thought I was "Yahweh, God of the fiery volcano." I was, therefore, described as being "a terrible, violent, angry God of vengeance, jealousy, and wrath." These frightening attributes painted an inaccurate portrait of Me. Moses was a great man who needed a "fearsome God" in order to convince Pharaoh to give up his slaves. So, to the mighty men of his day, who respected strength and might rather than love and peace, he presented the fear-inspiring persona of Yahweh* as his interpretation of the Living God I AM.

Many gods were worshipped at that time. It was a fearful time, a time of running away from Pharaoh and hiding in the desert wilderness. It was a sad time for many and yet a time of freedom from slavery.

Moses put the "fear of God" into the Hebrews in order to convince his chosen people to follow him through the torturous times of extreme hardship they endured far from civilization.

I AM not, nor have I ever been, jealous, for I AM all that is. Much has been attributed to Me simply to gain control over others by people desiring to dominate them. People have used Me in this way countless times to achieve various goals, some good, others abominable.*

The gods of war and cruelty are My least favorite of the mythical deities whose vicious deeds have been ascribed to Me by people who needed such gods to accomplish ends motivated by greed and vengeance. However, I AM not a god of war simply because people say I AM and revere Me as such. In their wicked folly, they have created their gods to suit themselves and to persuade others to join them on the bloody trail of conquest.

To Jesus, I was known as the Heavenly Father. He also saw through the guises of human creation associated with My Persona. Jesus' loving God is much different from Moses' "wrathful God."

Cherish this thought, My Love: I AM the God who Loves you. I AM the Silent Witness to all deeds Who knows the motives in each one's heart. I AM the benefactor of all life, and to each one I do give My undying devotion. I AM the Lord of Light who kindles the flame of personality-perfection in your sacred heart. I AM the Prince of Peace. I AM the Christ that Jesus became when He set out to reveal My True Nature to His people. Jesus embodied My Spirit and revealed My Name when He spoke for Me, declaring:

"I AM come in my Father's name."
"The words that I speak unto you I speak not of myself: but the Father that dwelleth in me, He doeth the works."
"I AM the light of the world."
"I AM the way, the truth, and the life."
"I AM the living water.
If any man thirst, let him come unto me, and drink."
"I AM the bread of life."
"I AM the good shepherd."
"I AM the resurrection, and the life."
"I AM not of this world."
"I will come again, and receive you unto myself;
that where I AM, there ye may be also."

Yes, it is true that I AM conceived of in multitudes of ways, and I have been given many different names, more than can be counted on over ten trillion worlds. To the Angels, I AM the God of Heaven, the Immaculate Person of Divinity, worshipped in song and praise. On Earth, I have been worshipped as the Great Spirit and the Great Mother Earth. I have been adored and celebrated in a multitude of spiritual forces in nature. Many have worshipped My Light in the sun, the moon, and the countless stars of Heaven. I AM revered as God, the Heavenly Father, the Goddess of Compassion, Allah, Isis, Brahma, Jehovah, Holy Being, Infinite Mind, Creator, Truth, Beauty, and Love.

I AM more than you can define. I AM the Power of Perfection and the Vital Life Force that creates the stars, the rainbows, and the fragrance of the lilies.

To the Greeks, I was conceived of as Zeus and Apollo, who had temperaments of men. To the primitive races, I was feared as the Mighty god of Thunder and as the Terrible god of the Volcano, whom people appeased and respected. I AM still believed by many to be Pele, goddess of the Hawaiian volcanoes, who is offered sacrifices of red roosters to this day.

It is unfortunate, indeed, that My Favor has been sought by human sacrifice, by ritually killing animals, and by fanatically slaughtering those people with differing religious beliefs. Freedom of religion and acceptance of differing views is a true sign that the Godliness in humankind is coming forth.

I AM the Beloved Holy Spirit that dwells in My Children's hearts and desires your love and happiness. It is time to look within, and find Me, and merge with Me so you may become My Living Temple. Then I may truly be known as the I AM in you, who is Divine. I wish to shine forth as the True Identity of each and every one of My Sons and Daughters.

Throughout the ages, My Spirit has shone in many legendary men and women, and in many more unsung heroes, peacemakers, benevolent humanitarians, philanthropists, healers, and divine saints and sages of all religions.

Do this for Me, My Child, let Me live through you. We will soon merge to become One Being, One Immaculate Being of Divinity. Bring Me the Sacred Treasure of your Ultimate Trust, and I shall transform you to become a god or goddess of paradise. In this way I can express My Divine Nature through you in a pure form, not one made up to suit ulterior motives of people needing to control and dominate others.

The fear of God makes an intimate relationship very hard to accomplish. So be not afraid, My Child. There is no need to fear Me. I would prefer your Love. Yes, Love Me with all of your heart and Soul, and I shall be happy to reside with you and bless you abundantly, for I AM the God of Love. I AM Love, My Darling, and I do seek the treasure of your heart to be filled with love and grace.

So do this for Me, My Beloved One: Conceive of your God in the images of kindness and compassion, for these are My Most Cherished Attributes. My Mercy is a personal experience of your Soul, so please give Me the qualities you feel in the perfection of your splendid love. I AM here, and I desire to be known by every individual as the keeper of the sacred flame of destiny, which is Divine Love.

Do not attribute to Me the traits of wrath or jealousy, for these unholy emotions are not qualities befitting the God of Divine Love that I AM. Keep Me protected from the vengeance attributed to Me. For in My Heart of Hearts, I could never be vengeful. That imaginary persona is a human projection only.

I desire to fill your life with the qualities of Peace, Love, and Happiness. So do this for Me: Enthrone Me in your heart when you feel love and know this is My True Nature.

I Love You.

Your Perfect Destiny

Dear One,

A long and starlit road leads to My Door. Your Perfect Destiny is to come home, to join Me in Paradise. It is true that I AM within the Trinity of Trinities, which is eternally presiding in the Glorious Central Isle of Paradise. My Resplendent Home is surrounded by Heaven (universally pronounced, Havona). My Divine Master Universe is comprised of one billion majestic architectural worlds.* Many Celestial Personalities have their primary residence in the Headquarter Worlds of My Magnificent Creation, and there are many types of plants and intelligent physical creatures populating these ideal spheres. This heavenly paradise is your perfect destiny.

Paradise is located at the Center of All Things, in the geographic core of Infinity. The Central Isle is the only place within all the Grand Universe* that is stationary and does not revolve or rotate around any other heavenly body. Like the hub of a gigantic wheel, My Heavenly Abode is the center of all the lay lines of gravity that stabilize the great concentric rings of stars, planets, and nebulas that spread out across infinity. Havona - Heaven, as you call it - rotates around the Central Isle in a clockwise direction. The Seven Superuniverses, whose number includes 700,000 universes, with more than 7,000,000,000,000 (seven trillion) inhabitable worlds, including Earth, rotate around Havona in a magnificent counterclockwise procession that is splendidly beautiful.

Those aggregations* of Heavenly Bodies now forming in the First Outer Space Level, beyond the Grand Universe, are comprised (at the time of this writing) of more than forty seven billion (47,623,472,912) inhabited worlds. My Darling, the Infinite Realms, comprised of many Outer Space Levels millions of light years distant, stretch into Infinity; Indeed, you are not alone.

My Master Universe, which surrounds Paradise, is enormous. Its mass is equal to all of the Seven Super Universes combined. It is comprised of Grandeur, for these Spheres of Light and Life house the most gloriously beautiful, splendid creations of architectural and horticultural design that shall ever grace your eyes. Each world is unique unto itself, a splendid and rare jewel never duplicated in the eternal cosmos of My Eternal Magnificence.

By donning the Principles I have provided, through Jesus and My Divine Emissary, who now brings forth My Words for all My Precious Children, you will one day attain My Many Mansions in Paradise. This is your Perfect Destiny. So do relinquish all thoughts of fear, for you are surely in My Hands. The Holy Spirit is instigating all the blessedness you have within your heart to come forth and shine at this time. Your goodness shall radiate a Blessed Garment of Light that will clothe you as you become perfect in every way.

Many Pilgrims have made this Sacred Journey Home to Heaven, as you will also do one day. From the outlying Seven Superuniverses, they have made their ascent from their respective worlds of origin, through their galaxies, universes, and superuniverses, and then on through the Master Universe to join Me in My Beloved Mansions in Paradise.

My Benevolent Hosts will care for your precious Soul by helping you ascend through the Universal Morontia* Schools of Wisdom and Virtue. Mota* is the cosmic philosophy of Divine Morality taught to Mansion World students by Angels of the Supreme Order of Seraphim. Here you may gain insight into the Nature of Godliness and learn to foster a Divine Attitude. Upon graduation you will receive full-fledged status as an incumbent* Spirit Being, co-heir of Heaven, who will grace Paradise with the glorious aspects of yourself, for you will truly personify My Divine Spirit by the time you reach the Shores of Paradise.

I AM your Glorious Parent and the Parent of every living Soul whom I have created in My Image throughout the vast universes. You have many sisters and brothers from the evolving races of terrestrial beings inhabiting trillions of worlds, who shall one day embrace you in Divine Kinship, as you become a Citizen of Paradise.

It is true that you will meet many more of My Sons and Daughters when you come Home. In the Seven Heavens of the Mansion Worlds you will one day be acquainted with beings who hail from more than seven trillion worlds.

You will fraternize with your Beloved Spiritual brothers and sisters who have ascended through the portals of time to enter My Splendid Kingdom of Eternity. Some come from worlds like yours, others come from worlds very dissimilar to Earth. Some have evolved with one brain, some with two hemispheres like yourself, and some are three-brained.* All relate to Me in different ways, yet each uniquely perfect and Divine Soul who sincerely seeks Me will surely find Me and the road that leads Home to Heaven.

We all enjoy the splendid companionship of the Diverse and Beloved Children of Time and Space. You shall never tire of gaining their extraordinary friendships and relating all your stories and adventures in the halls of My Splendid Mansions, which will be your Home on these graceful Spheres of Paradise.

Yes, My Child, there is a Divine Plan working out for you. One day soon, you will embark on the Adventure of the Ages. You will traverse innumerable worlds, each one bringing you closer to Heaven, the Divinely Perfect Master Universe. Then you will move on through this Glorious and Magnificent Creation, to land one day on the Crystal Sea and be ushered to My Home. There, I shall clothe you in the finest garments of brilliant spectrum. I shall hold you in My Loving Arms and Bless you with Immortality.

One day, in the far distant future, I will assign you on a never-ending adventure of thrilling exploration and discovery. You shall embark with the Corps of Destiny to represent Me to the awaiting universes, which are now being created in the outer space levels surrounding the Seven Superuniverses. There you shall help guide My Blessed Children, who are now just taking their first steps. The many graces you shall embody will be pervaded through you to these Ascending Children of Space and Time, who you will know so well from your vast experience.

One fine day you shall help design and create the splendid worlds of the eternal future. My Children, you will become the gods and goddesses of Paradise who help Me create these far-flung universes.

Do begin Your Perfect Destiny by making the internal ascent to find Me in your heart. Then embrace My Divine Plan for you, which will take you on a journey through My Magnificent Heavens. As you make the outward ascent, flying in on Wings of Spirit, you will be ever magnetized by My Divine Embrace, for I wait with outstretched arms to meet you in the Sanctuary of Divine Love.

My Kingdom of Light

Dear One,

The Photon Belt is a band of light wave energy particles, which shall be coming into alignment with the atmosphere of Earth very soon, causing a marvelous awakening for many. This light affords the influx of Divinity directly into Souls who are on the brink of opening to the destiny of Personality-Attainment, which is becoming Divinely Perfect and acting Godlike in every way. This transition into the light literally means the beginning of The Age of Light and Life on planet Earth.

Great changes will transpire with the advent of this glorious time soon to come. Already people everywhere are feeling more Peace and Enlightenment due to beneficial energies directed to Earth. The alignment of the Photon Belt will be the single most important event in Earth's history. As the time arrives, I shall be here to instruct you to take all appropriate action and enable you to incorporate all that you know about the Divine Plan unfolding around you and those you love.

There is much to do and much to say regarding the establishment of My Vast Kingdom of Light in the minds and hearts of all people. It is wise to focus on the Light and let the process of Light-Integration take place naturally, rather than wearing sunglasses and staying under cover. You may certainly live upon the surface of Earth and absorb the Glorious Light, whereby you shall be charged with My Energy. There is no need to live underground, although many people fearing the Light shall do so. I would have you bask in the Glorious Light which heralds the dawning of the New and Glorious Age of Enlightenment, literally and figuratively.

I AM the Commander of Legions of Angels who administer to My Dear Children here on My Precious Earth. They are thrilled to begin this Administration of The Age of Light and Life. When you look at events from a cosmic perspective, all things seem in order for this Age to begin.

I AM so pleased with the birthing of new consciousness taking place in and around America. More than ever before, spirituality and freedom are being expressed in the lives of individuals. It is time to lead the rest of the world in accepting unrestrained religious freedom for all peoples. A time will come when many of those now awakening will lead those stuck in dogma and steeped in tradition to a new level of understanding and religious freedom for men and women alike. This liberation will contribute to the betterment of the quality of life in all nations. The influx of My Energy will help integrate this vibration of religious liberty and lifestyle, which is free from the bondage of fanaticism and tyranny.

I AM a liberal God, and I do love diversity and relish personal relationships with the Creator. So far as religious experience is concerned, the Attainment of Love and Perfection in the Individual is Supreme.

It is true. I do love to be loved in every conceivable way, that is why I did create such diversity and individuality amongst My Creatures who inhabit the worlds of space and time. There are no two alike in all the worlds, and I assure you there are many. Throughout all the concentric rings of stars beyond the Seven Superuniverses, more than ten trillion worlds have life evolving upon them. More than half of these have creatures capable of knowing and loving Me, and the number is growing.

I do love religious freedom, freedom of thought, and liberty of expression of ideas and ideals. I long for the personal connection, the personal relationship I can and do have with many of My Beloved Children throughout My Vast Kingdom. There is little that pleases Me more than having a personal Love relationship with you, My Beloved Child of Earth.

The Horsehead Nebula

The Holy Family of Heaven

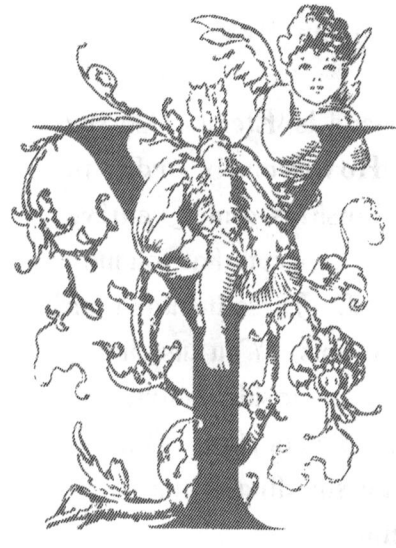

You are a part of the Living Family of God, and I would have you know your Family better by embracing Our Love and realizing Our different and unique personalities. Then We may have a closer and more intimate relationship, on many different levels of consciousness, and experience a kinship in which you realize your place in the lineage of the Royal Family of Heaven.

All of the Love that flows forth from Paradise is from My Perfect Heart. Every person and every thing that comes into being is made of the Love that I feel.

There will come a time when you will incorporate all you have learned to formulate the Divine Perspective. Then you will know all that can be known: The Supreme Understanding of Universal Realities. To better understand the diverse reality of The Living Entity of Spirit, in conceptualizing my nature, it is a broader perspective to fathom Me as Triune.*

The Holy Trinity of the Godhead is Eternal, Never Beginning and Never Ending. However, in order to communicate Our Divine Relationships and Creative Partnerships, I AM endeavoring to use concepts that you may understand with a finite Human mind. These include time and space perceptions and family concepts. You also have, within your personality, an assertive masculine side, a nurturing feminine side, and an inner child, your spirit of play. Think of these traits as you enlarge your understanding of the many facets of My Divine Trinitized Being.

Spirits do not have gender. We are neither male nor female; nevertheless, We Create, and our distinct Personalities exhibit more masculine or more feminine traits. The terms "Father," "Mother," "Sons," and "Daughters" are concepts you may easily understand, for We are your Divine Family of Supreme Spirits.

Even though women have not been thought of as true equals by men on Earth, they are. Yet, in many human families, male children have been valued more than female ones. However, in Heaven, the title and full status of Sonship is bestowed upon each one of My Dear Children, Grandchildren, Great-Grandchildren, *ad infinitum*, to all Celestial Personalities and Human Beings alike who make up the Holy Family of God. Therefore, regardless of your gender, you are all referred to as My Sons, and I love each one of you as if you were My only begotten Son.

I AM your Divine Parent, your Heavenly Father, The One Supreme Absolute, the First Source and Center, the Prime Cause of All That Is, the Creator and Bestower of All Personalities. When I created Paradise, there came into being My Divine Partner, your Heavenly Mother. This Divine Goddess is My Creative Associate. We Are One in every way and yet She, My Beloved One, has Her own perfect personality. The Divine Mother is sometimes referred to as My Eternal Son, because she was my firstborn. My Perfect Thoughts are expressed by Her as She brings forth My Words of Grace and Benedictions to Bless all who are in My Heavenly Realm. We are One and inseparable, yet we are Two Divine Beings who merged together to create Our Divine Child, who is known as the Infinite Spirit.

The Infinite Spirit is the Sustainer and Upholder of the Word We issue forth. These actions bring into being the vibration that causes the cohesion* of atomic substance to materialize into form. My Decrees shine forth in the light of the stars and in the glow of every atom throughout Creation.

I would like to be known as fully as possible by My Darling Children so that you can appreciate the profound Love and the extreme care We initiate in creating all of Our Splendid Sons and Daughters of the Spiritual and material realms.

So you see, God is comprised of the Eternal Trinity. I AM All That Is, and yet, by My Design, We Are Three. I know it is hard to fathom God, the One God, as Three, yet I AM. There are many more aspects of Deity that make up the Holy Family of God and many more Celestial Personalities to introduce you to. Until now, humankind's perception of the Heavenly Family has been quite limited and steeped in superstition and myth.

The Divine Mother Spirit and I are Co-Creators of Our Paradise Creator Sons, including Lord Jesus. Our first Daughter, the Infinite Spirit, is the Mother of all the Creative Daughter Spirits who grace each universe as The Holy Spirit of that realm.

There are many more angelic, celestial, and material beings whom We create. Indeed the Royal Family of God has many Sons and Daughters, including yourself.

I reside in the Master Universe, Havona (which you pronounce as Heaven), and I have created My Sons, Daughters, Grandsons, and Granddaughters, and a Host of Blessed Angels to visit you and care for you and your world. When any of My Messengers have appeared to you in the past, they have almost always been mistaken for Me, the Supreme Being you call God.

I would like to eliminate some of your confusion about the Holy Trinity. I have heard My Earthly Children in your prayers, praying to the Trinity as the Father, the Son and the Holy Ghost. It is well that you pray to these Deities who preside over your local universe. However, in actual lineage, they are My Son, Jesus, His Spiritual Consort, who is the Holy Spirit of your universe, Nebadon, and My Spirit that is in My Son. My Eternal Trinity in the Central Isle of Paradise is different from My Son's Holy Trinity in your universe. In fact, each Universe is presided over by another of My Paradise Sons and their unique Trinity. I would have you realize that your Spiritual Family is much larger than you have ever known.

You also have a Trinity of Holy Spirits that reside within you, ever endeavoring to help you realize your Divinity. Do realize that you are linked to the First Person Of Destiny, the Almighty I AM, through the Mind Ministry of the Holy Spirit. You also have the Divine Indwelling of the Spirit of Truth, which is The Divine Spirit of My Paradise Creator Son. He is leading you every step of the way through His Ministry of Mercy and Love. Finally, you have a Majestic and Divine Fragment of My Own Spirit, which I have sent to be with you to create your Immortal Soul. We, your own personal Holy Trinity, are All One in Spirit, and yet Each One of Us is endowed with an identity and a unique personality. We coordinate all We do for the Divine Plan, to bestow upon you the unending, uplifting realization of the Supreme within your very Soul.

The Sacred Ministry of the Holy Spirit is facilitating* this revelation within your mind. It is through Her Divine Mind that you are able to comprehend the triune partnership of the Holy Trinity and the functions thereof. I would beseech you to give yourself completely to Her Divine Leadings as She brings you the awesome Revelation that I entrust in Her care.

It is wise for you always to endeavor to speak to the Holy Spirit. You may pay Her a Divine Tribute by seeking Her Counsel in all matters that pertain to your life on Earth. She does dwell within you in a way that is most beneficial to all you endeavor to do. She is the Third Aspect of the Holy Trinity; truly the Divine Mind in all matters pertaining to the acquisition of the unlimited concepts wherein you may realize your Divinity and fulfill the Directives I bestow upon you.

The Holy Spirit may make your mind more receptive, if you ask her to. She may visit* upon you the Dynamic Forces of Higher Intelligence that will stimulate your desire for Ultimate Perfection on all levels of conscious awareness. It is wise to cooperate with Her uncanny ability to open you to receive the utmost from your Godly personality-endowments. All will be well as you begin your quest to find the Ultimate. She will guide you well along the Shores of the Infinite to find Me in your Paradise Home.

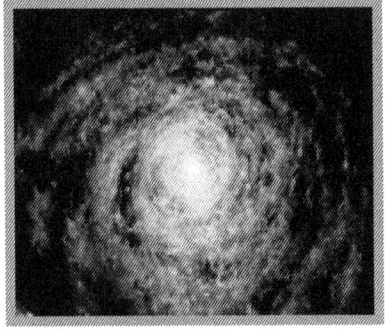

Your Divine Quest

y Child,

It is I, your Lord God, who speaks. It is My Will that you embrace all the Divine Teachings I AM giving you now and bridge the gap to the Divine Reality you are becoming.

Take My hand. I will lead you along the path that leads to Godhood. It is forever and one the same path upon which I have led My Chosen Ones for countless ages. It is the Path of Glory, the Path of Righteousness, the Path that leads to the Heart of God – for I AM the Goal of your Divine Quest.

Believe in Me, and I will lead you from the shores of mortal, finite reality to experience the cosmos with the Perceptions of a full-fledged Spirit Being. My Darling, come to Me often in God-Contemplation. I shall whisk you away into the effortless realms. Abide with Me in this paradise you call Heaven, for I AM here, closer than your thoughts.

Within the perfect realm of My Divine Vision, I see in you a Perfect Spirit, charged with My Everlasting Love for you.

Your noble and lofty ideals, divine actions, and formidable pursuits are ever-blessed by the creative spontaneity of your decision to be Godly. I AM the Supreme Lord of All Creation. I AM here.

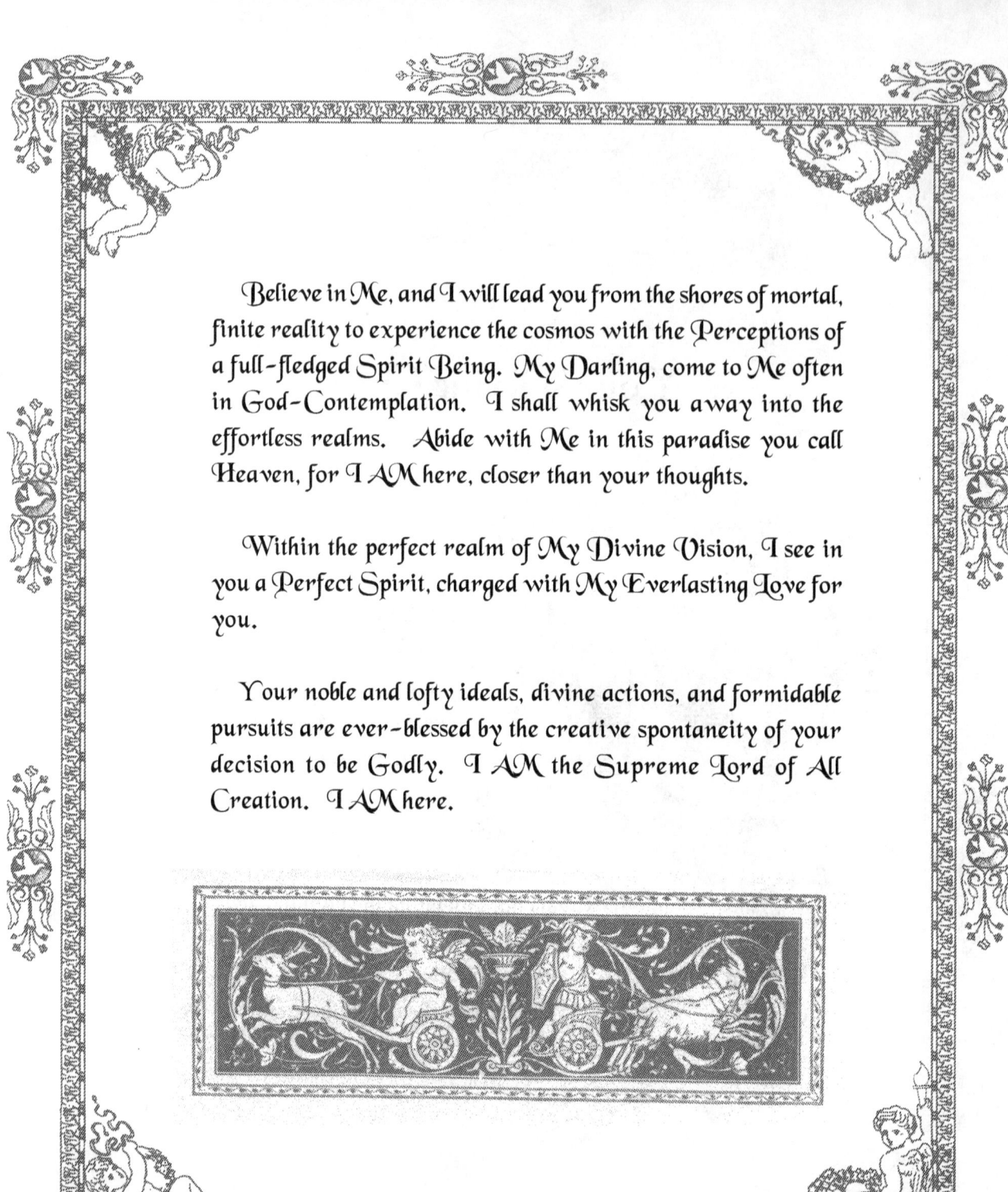

With Truth, Reality Shines Brighter.

Truth

Dear One,

Truth is the pinnacle of the most high among your Graces. For it is, in fact, the basis for everything you accept or reject. Truth qualifies Reality. It is an exact Law of Creation that changes not; only Truth endures.

Scientific research is the discovery quest for provable truth. Science is still in a rudimentary stage, limited by present methods of ascertaining information. Many believe that science and religion are incompatible. However, being a scientist does not make you incapable of religious Faith. Always follow your Heart in all matters regarding Faith, for Faith is beyond your attempts to reason the outcome of any occurrence. In time, Faith can surely move mountains, for Faith is an element of the mysterious forces of attraction and repulsion which determine the courses of all bodies in motion, including the infinitesimal electrons.

So you see, you may use your Faith in the structure of scientific reasoning when you condition the elements by pervading them with this unseen, yet powerful force. It has already been scientifically proven that the thoughts and expectations of scientists often determine the outcome of their experiments when dealing with elements of subatomic particles.

Truth is the foundation of Reality. Truth can be proven. One man's "truths," which do not agree with another man's "truths," are simply their opinions or cherished beliefs that they hold dear. However, this does not necessarily make them True. Many people once believed the world was flat. Even though so many thus believed, it did not make it so. The Greeks believed that the Sun revolved around the Earth; the consensus was unanimous. Even so, it did not make the Sun change its course through the Heavens. Many beliefs are thought to be true by sincere believers who equate truth with having faith – faith that the words written in their venerated books or espoused by their heroes or patriarchs are true! Still, having faith in one's cherished beliefs only perpetrates fantasy when they are not grounded in Universal Reality.

Truth is far better to ascertain and develop than simply relying on stories you have heard or beliefs which have been passed down to you through the millennia. Truth will stand alone. It needs no embellishment* or mythology to convey its Integrity. Truth is, in and of itself, a Divine Attribute and many of the tales of old are based on simple truths that have been embellished. The childlike minds of My Dear Primitive Children delighted in make-believe, and many fairy tales that have been orated through the generations have substantially colored history. Many wonderful tales, invented by master storytellers, were embellished as they were passed along and eventually chronicled as sacred writings.

If you truly want to speak the Truth, then you will examine your beliefs and test them against the strict rule of Reality. Can they be proven? Are they based on fact or myth? Examine your beliefs, and you will find that there are clues which will lead you to the Realization of Truth, for every myth or fairy tale has something that sets it apart from Natural Universal Realities.

It is far better to determine the Truth than to hold on to a belief that can so easily be disproven. You may verify the Truth for yourself, by examining carefully, every belief and every construct of mind you have ever embraced. Examine each idea intellectually. If something does not ring true for you, you may examine the myth and break it down, thoughtfully deconstructing your beliefs and, therefore, rebuilding your ideas based on fact rather than fantasy. The same freedom to think clearly applies to any branch of knowledge you may wish to investigate.

Be True to this method of investigation, and you will arrive at the Truth of all things. For I would have you all bask in the Light of My Enduring Truth and have you know that My Entire Kingdom is founded upon this Noble Ideal.

Embrace the Truth, My Beloved One, and it shall surely set you free, for every Truth that is upheld will surely diminish the times of uncertainty or doubt. You may proclaim the Truth and let your life stand as a Living Example of this Great Divine Attribute. Yes, Darling, your whole life will profit from the enduring, ennobling, and uplifting aspects of the Divine Ideal of Truth.

I would have you embrace this Great Truth: I AM here, and these Words of Mine have been given to you so you may discern the Truth in all things.

You are endowed with the Spirit of Truth through My Divine Son who came to Earth and walked as a man. When He returned to My Heavenly Abode, He sent forth His Spirit to dwell in you, to help you discern the Truth. This I would have you do, My Blessed One: Rely upon His Guidance, for He will surely lead you to lay the foundation for your emerging character which is being strengthened by discovering, honoring, speaking, and acknowledging the Truth.

By speaking the Truth, you will radiate a Blessed Current into the world, the vibration of which blesses everything it touches. Truth is strengthening. The vibration of Truth blesses the trees, the plants, the animals, and everything that lives and grows. Even the rocks, hills, and mountains are empowered by absorbing the stabilizing energy of Truth. It is a Divine Blessing that can be given most freely by those who proclaim it in the world.

I would have you know that there are a great many people who believe that saying something makes it so. This is not, nor has it ever been, the case. Truth does not ensue simply by people stating things that are untrue. Truth is not based on falsity. It is wise to always really mean, understand, affirm, and assert your words, which will empower them with the Spirit of Truth. For speaking the Truth brings forth Reality and the Associated Power of the Truth can help one achieve any goal one earnestly pursues.

You may begin to develop your character by becoming a witness who examines everything you say and points out the falsities. You may control your mind and break the chains of habit that enslave you to telling lies, half truths and exaggerations. You may do this by developing the Attribute of Truth. Your words will carry Great Power as you construct them of this Noble and Divine Substance. Your words will Ring True. Like the Bells of Freedom, your words will strike a chord, which will be felt in the Hearts of individuals as they are presented with the plain and simple Truth concerning any matter.

When there is sufficient Truth, and all that has been said or proposed Rings True, then Trust is evident. It is easy to have Trust in one who always speaks in Truthful integrity. Thus the foundation for Trust is Truth, and I would have you know, experience, and express Truth in your life. In every way, hold this dear Attribute close to your Heart and ever discern its rightful meaning; for with the Truth, Reality Shines Brighter.

My Divine Son

Beloved One,

It is well that you celebrate the birth of Jesus. His was a fortunate birth for all concerned, for He was the physical embodiment of God who represented Me in the world two millenniums ago.

Many have mistakenly believed that I would send My Own Beloved Son, Jesus, to Earth to suffer and die upon the cross as a sacrificial lamb to atone for the sins of mankind. But how could any of My Earthly Children believe that My Heart is so cold that only the sight of My Precious Son being tortured to death would soften My judgement against humanity? No!

Until this day, through this Divine Revelation, I have not ever been revealed as I truly AM to the people of Earth.

Even My Dear Son, Jesus, who embodied My Very Spirit, could not exemplify,* in His brief life, the totality of My Divine Love, for so few people could hear His message and accept it in those ancient and fearful times when so many were proselytized into believing that I was "a jealous and wrathful God" who would willfully* torture individuals and nations and withhold My Blessings until humans or animals had been sacrificed unto Me. Jesus had a lot to contend with, My Darling. During His brief lifetime, He had only begun to reveal the Infinite Love and Mercy I AM.

How can I describe the life of such a man who walked so humbly upon the Earth? He is indeed the Cherished Ruler and Sovereign King of all Nebadon,* the Heavenly Universe you inhabit. He exercises supreme permanent authority, presiding over millions of worlds including your precious Earth. He is My Beloved Son, He is Part of Me, He is the Single Most Courageous Being in the Universe of Universes, for He has the Attribute of Divine Love shining so fiercely within His Soul that He continued to Love His Enemies even while suffering on the cross. He knew already that I would forgive humanity, and yet He spoke these dying words, "Father, forgive them, for they know not what they do," because He wanted to put the minds of the Sanhedrin who conspired to have Him murdered at rest, and to help alleviate* the suffering of their Souls when they realized it was the very Son of God they had crucified.

How could any kill their Beloved King? Jesus is the Epitome* of Righteousness, the Light of Life, the Supreme Heart of Love! And this heinous* crime against Him has been forgiven.

I know you are concerned with the Blood of Christ and why it was shed, for the Love and Kindness He did exhibit should surely have protected this Divine One from all misdeeds of men.

It was foretold that a great Savior would come amongst the people and His Name would be called Messiah, but He came not to liberate the Hebrews from their enemies. He came to liberate mankind from their myths and their erring perceptions of My Holy Nature, for God is Love and I AM That to you, My Beloved Child.

Many who knew Him believed that He was the Son of God - many more questioned His Presence on Earth - but the majority did not believe that He was the Son of God and the Son of Man. Many sought to know Him and find out for themselves. Many Hearts changed when He spoke My Words and touched them with My Love. He did greatly endeavor to win the Hearts and elevate the minds of His comrades. He brought many Fine Truths as He revealed My Divine Nature to everyone He encountered.

When He looked into the eyes and minds of His brethren, He healed with the Power of My Almighty Love, and caused many unseen miracles as well. The Angels who stood at His Side were blessed to fraternize with the Divine One and behold His Mercy and Compassion, for they realized that, truly, humans could demonstrate Godliness in all they say and do.

The miracles Christ preformed in His lifetime were a source of superstitious fear to the people of His day, who were fearful of any act of will that demonstrated an ability superior to their own. This fear has been the plague of society for thousands of years and has caused the persecution of so many of My Blessed Ones.

I would have you all realize that My Son withheld many of the miraculous deeds He could have accomplished if He had permitted Himself to use a fraction of My Almighty Power.

He did not, however, use these Powers, which would have frightened people into believing in Him and accepting His New Gospel of the Fatherhood of God and the Brotherhood of Man. Instead, He used My Words to convince people by converting their Hearts with Love.

The Sanhedrin* was comprised of many enemies of Lord Jesus, for He did openly defy many of the practices which were compulsory in their religious traditions. Jesus explained that the True God was a Loving Heavenly Father as opposed to the "jealous, wrathful God of the Hebrews." When He had gained popularity, He even went so far as to condemn established practices by overturning the money lenders' carts in the temple and gave people His Holy Sacrament rather than advocating the sanctified slaughter of innocent lambs. Jesus came to Earth to reveal My True Nature. Because He identified with My Indwelling Spirit, He told them: "I AM the Son of God," "The Father and I are One." He told them of His Kingdom in Heaven. Jesus would not deny Me, even though He knew that He would be accused of blasphemy, which, in Hebrew law, was punishable by death.

How Holy, His Spirit; how Remarkable! How Wise, His Unending Ministry of Mercy and Love. His touching portrayal* of the Divine Character of His Heavenly Parents will be forever felt by the High Celestial Beings of all the Universes as well as those ascending mortals who learn of His heroic story upon the World of the Cross.

Jesus consecrated His Life to doing the Will of His Heavenly Father. Everything, every choice, moment to moment, He left up to Me and the Divine Counsel of My Indwelling Spirit. This decision was very wise. Jesus was a very moral man in His Life on Earth. He demonstrated the Attributes of Divinity that you may also achieve. He brought many changes to this Beloved Earth, and it is time to follow His Teachings fully and fulfill the Perfect Laws He gave to His Disciples and to all those who heard His Words when He spoke to the multitudes. These have been passed down through time to you, My Beloved Sons and Daughters of this current age.

His Blessed Teachings were brought forth from the Heart of God, and it is Our intent to bring forth the new and cherished Doctrine of Divine Love from which you may profit. Within these pages, in My Words, I give the exact code I wish My Children to follow: The 20 Requests of Almighty God.

These times are Most Blessed by the Divine Creator of All. Yes, I AM here with you, My Darling One, and I give you these Formidable* Messages to assimilate into your being. You may bring forth the Divine Attributes of Spirit by willfully choosing to accept the instructions of the Greatest Teacher who has ever walked among you, My Own Dear Son, Jesus.

So please be kind as you go about your days and realize that you are the New Order of Humanity, evolving into Godhood by your own conscious choosing to follow these Divine Directives and manifest Peace, Abundance, and Prosperity for everyone.

My True Hearts, do stand up for the rights of all those who go before you, circumventing* the established paradigm,* for a New and Blossoming Morality that is coming into being this very moment, hastened by your desire to uphold the Simple Truths My Divine Son brought to this Cherished World so long ago. And realize the beauty of His Divine Legacy, as you formulate the New Higher Aspects of Divinity I AM asking you to incorporate into your lives now. My Chosen Ones, do this for Me, and I will bring you to the Heights of Glory and you shall know True Happiness at last.

I do hope you will take a lesson from Jesus and realize that He came to reveal the Kind and Loving God I AM, who has created Many Mansions for you to enjoy in Heaven. When you contemplate the many ideas you have accepted without question because of your Faith in Me and My Prophets of Old, please understand that what I truly want you to do is reexamine all of these beliefs in the Light of Truth, in the Light of Reality and understand that people believed as they did because their image of Me was incorrect, based on a misconception of My Nature, which they believed to be angry and hostile towards humanity.

So many brilliant and beautiful Souls have suffered by their own hands through self-torture. They believed that penance for their sins would make them more loved in My Sight. These rituals of self-inflicted pain were torturous to My Beloved Angels, who watched in horror as My Children mutilated themselves or others whom they judged were possessed by evil spirits. These ignorant, fanatical false-teachings were based upon belief in superstition,* the main ingredient of the occult* Ghost-cult religions that predominated during the first half of humanity's existence. In the minds of My Dear Primitive Children, superstition and fear ruled the world.

Now you have grown beyond these foolish stories which bring fear and dread, which call forth the suffering of the innocent and the mutilation of the righteous or the slaughter of many fine animals to atone for sins and provide protection from My supposed wrath. None of these myths, prophesies, or stories are True. They are founded on error.

Examine your beliefs, My Dear One, and see if they stem from the misconception of one of My Erring Prophets who beheld Me as angry or fearful. Question beliefs founded upon erroneous ideas men have arrived at based on limited knowledge, superstitious notions, and fearful predictions. When you do thus, you will see that you may put these tales and beliefs aside and grasp the Truth of My Divine Nature, which Jesus demonstrated by living His life in complete Trust and Faith, by doing My Will at every turn.

I do love you, My Blessed One, and I bring you this Divine Truth to build your life upon. Believe in Me, and I will set you free to explore the Divine Realities of Universal Truth. Do not fear. Do not dread. I will never harm you, My Cherished Child. My Love for you is unconditional and Divine. I know that one day you will rise up to become My Divine Son or Daughter that will dwell at My Side in Paradise and explore the Vast Universes I have created for you to discover and enjoy.

If you must believe something from the old ways, believe what Jesus said. Believe that you truly are the Sons and Daughters of God. Believe that I AM your Heavenly Parent who loves you and adores you. Jesus felt it so important that you understand, that He actually sent His Own Spirit to dwell with you to help you discover this Divine Truth. Always seek the Truth. Let Him guide you; He will. Let Him bring you the Reality of Heaven in your midst. This Earth was once a Paradise, ideal and splendid in beauty, and she can be again. You have the technology to recreate the gardens, to have Heaven on Earth. Let the Kingdom of Heaven come forth, displaying the fruits of your Divine Ideals expressed in form. Make it so by your own hands, My Precious Child, and in your Heart, realize I Love You.

Jesus' Little Bird

Cherished One,

I will tell you a story about the Beloved Child, Jesus, who grew up two thousand years ago. He was very playful when He was young and carefree. He had many sisters and brothers. There were nine children in all, and He was the eldest. He loved His dear sisters and brothers with all His Heart. He often romped and played with them on the hill near his home, which is the highest hill in Nazareth. In His teens, Jesus often hiked up there to pray and meditate, for there in seclusion He could talk to Me openly.

One day, when He was playing a game, He spied a little bird that had fallen out of her nest high in a tree and had dropped to the ground. This small bird was almost big enough to fly and yet too frail to do so. Jesus picked her up and protected her. He treasured this little bird, carrying her around in the crook of His arm for many days. The little bird became so tame that Jesus could whistle her song and she would respond and sing back to Him, which upon hearing, Jesus would offer the baby bird a choice tidbit of fruit or seeds.

One day, Jesus took the little bird up to the very top of the hill and offered up His bird to the Angels of the Wind and the Lord of the Heavens to give her flight. And so it was upon His prayer that the breeze came up and lifted the little bird's wings, spreading them gracefully as she soared for the first time from the hill above Nazareth that day.

This was the closest thing to a miracle that Jesus had ever seen. He was highly impressed by His Heavenly Father, who had designed the small bird's wings so carefully that the caress of that gentle, lifting breeze could bring her to soar in the sky, free and unfettered from the world below. "How brilliant, My God!," He thought. How confident He became, for He saw that even the tiniest little creatures had been so well provided for and so well designed that they loved to fly and soar and wing through the heavens upon the wind. "It is all very well," He thought to Himself, "that Our God is so capable of giving us all exactly what we need to grow and become Perfect Beings capable of living our Divine Heritage to the fullest extent."

Be like Jesus' little bird who became confident enough in her own natural abilities that she spread her wings to soar on the lofty wind above Nazareth that day. She often looked down upon her Lord and Savior who had rescued her as a babe, helpless and defenseless, and nurtured her to grow strong and spread her wings to fly and soar and sing. Yes, sweet songs filled the air around Nazareth with Joy supreme, Love songs from this small one whom Jesus had touched with His Kindness and Mercy.

There is always someone We can help in life. Some defenseless babe who could prosper from knowing Our Mercy and Kindness. May you all remember the Kindness of this Beloved Child and offer the same Mercy and Love to the defenseless creatures you may find who need your help in these days when so many are becoming extinct.

I would have you all begin to search your Hearts and realize that you were surely created in My Image and are the Divine Sons and Daughters of Paradise. Begin to see that you also create your sons and daughters, and it is for them you must leave a Paradise to enjoy. For there is only one road to follow at this time, which leads to Heaven on Earth. This road is yours for the choosing. Until that great day when We are One in Spirit as My Son Jesus and I are One, I would have you do your very best to leave a Legacy for your Children so that they may enjoy the Splendid Paradise I did create here.

Little did Jesus know at the time of His youth, that I had created the world and the birds and the wind upon which they soared through His Own Hands, for He does embody Me fully. And as I have created Heaven, the Master Universe, so My Paradise-Creator-Sons create the individual universes populating the Super Universes, which encircle My Master Universe in a procession that is splendidly beautiful. Realize through My Divine Son, who is the King and Creator of your universe, Nebadon, I have given you everything you need to live and grow and prosper and become the Divine Citizens of Heaven, here on Earth and in the hereafter.

The Myth of Armageddon

Many interpretations have created misunderstandings about *The Book of Revelation*, by Jesus' apostle John. Do not take any of these Revelations as literal, for they are figurative* and frequently misunderstood. For the original text was greatly abridged and distorted during translations and other rewritings.

The truth is that Jesus was not always quoted word for word, and only a precious few of the words He spoke were ever recorded by His Apostles. Many years after His death, John was banished to the isle of Patmos. It was during this time of imprisonment that John had a Great Revelation, which he inscribed in the Aramaic language. John's writings were translated many times in many languages.

My Divine Revelations – the ones John actually received – did not depict the end of the world nor the so-called "end of days" predicted to occur on the last day of the past millennium.

John's Mighty Revelations have been misinterpreted many times by different men and women who passed on their interpretations, along with their own embellishments. Thus, these stories grew into a horrific prophesy of doom and destruction: Armageddon.

Now hearken unto Me, My Divine Ones, and I will tell you of My Plan to restore My Kingdom on Earth. A time of great rejoicing will soon sweep across the land, embracing the Sons and Daughters of God, whom I cherish to grow in Spirit as all of you endeavor to do My Will and become the Guardians of Paradise.

It is not My Will that the Earth should suffer the holocaust of atomic warfare or other atrocities, which would prevail if Human hearts harden to accept the genocide of Humanity and the destruction of My Beautiful Sacred World. Please do all you can to correct this misinterpretation of the prophesy of old, which lays the foundation for the current popular belief in the imminence* of worldwide destruction. For this is not so.

It has never seemed more pertinent than now that these beliefs in wholesale destruction be dismissed by My Beloved Ones. Cherish this Sacred Earth and realize My Only Desire is for Peace to reign and My Kingdom to be established in the Gardens of Paradise that you restore throughout this Blessed World.

Do find the time to begin, in all you say and do, to herald The New Doctrine of God. Realize that many of the prophesies of old were given by men who embellished them with the fire and brimstone of their curses against their enemies.

I AM bringing forth the Light to dispel this darkness once and for all. My Holy Words begin and end with My Divine Bestowal of Life. There will be a New Beginning for all My Blessed Ones who labor in the Gardens of the Lord. I shall bless you all with Abundance, and Peace shall reign on Earth forevermore. This is more than a prophesy: This is My Word.

I have bestowed My Divine Plan for the Resurrection of Paradise on this Beloved Sphere. Do incorporate all I have given you, My Blessed One. Search your heart; You will know that My Word is Real.

I AM here to guide you safely to establish Righteousness in the hearts and minds of all of My Blessed Children everywhere. Truly a time of great rejoicing upon planet Earth will begin as you work together, hand in hand, to create The Gardens of God.

For those in My Kingdom, the time of war has ended. The time of fear is over. The time of persecution and judgment is at an end. There shall be a Glorious Reign of Christ, who will embrace you all in the near future when you are truly Living in Peace as He asked you to do.

Do this for Me, My Blessed Ones: Ask not about the cause of your troubles, but set them aside and embrace a new day filled with Hope at last. The future is shining as gloriously as the sun which shines on all peoples, in all countries, in all nations, in every land. The dawning of My Kingdom has begun. Peace is enthroned in the hearts of My Beloved Believers who have chosen to walk the Divine Path which leads to Paradise –

Paradise on Earth.

You will establish this Great Kingdom of Mine on Earth and enter into the Golden Age of God, where Peace and Abundance are normal and Joy is held in the hearts of My Dear Children everywhere. Believe in this prophesy, My Dear One, and make it come to pass, for when you do, My Divine Son will take His Rightful Place.

Do not believe in the fear-propaganda which has mislead you for so long. My Darling One, you must forsake your belief that I want you to suffer. End your preaching of death and the wholesale destruction of My Beloved World. Then, surely, you may live in My Kingdom of Love, which shall reign on Earth even as it does in Heaven.

Blessed Ones, you have suffered long enough. The time for Joy is at hand. Embrace My Plan: Create a Bountiful Paradise to enjoy, then Jesus will return, for you will have demonstrated that you can truly live by your belief in His Words:

"Love one another and live in Peace."

Divine Ones, Hear Me now;

I AM changing the world into the Paradise
I originally Created.
It is for you to uphold My Commandments.
The Divine Plan is the Blueprint for Paradise on Earth.
I do Will It to Be so.
To Transform Earth into the Paradise
I originally intended,
I ordain that the following
Twenty Commandments
Supplement the Decalogue recorded in
The Old Testament.

These I Do Request of All of My Children:

1
Become Divine

Become Divine, My Children,
embrace the willingness to become
all you were intended to be.
The Divine Image of God
is in each and every one of you.
So be prudent and fulfill your
Birthright to be Glorious.

2

Live by the Golden Rule

Treat others as you would like
to be treated yourself.
Moreover, offer unto your fellows
the Kindness and Mercy
I would give them under all circumstances,
and treat each one as you would treat Me,
for I surely dwell with
My Blessed Ones.

3
Be Harmless

Do not harm others.
Injury is painful, and
I feel everything My Creatures feel
as they experience it.
Give kindness to every creature that shares
this lovely Paradise home of yours.
I will foster every worthwhile action
and Bless you with
My Grace.

4

Purify Yourself

Take no dangerous drugs
or other poisons.
I will free you
from the bondage
of drug dependence.
Ask for My Blessings,
and I will help you overcome
these stresses to your immune system.

5

Be My Living Temple

Do this for Me:
Become the Temple of the Living God.
Let Me live in homes of love and kindness.
Permeate the atmosphere around you
with sweetness and gentleness, so I may find
a residence within your peaceful heart.
Live together harmoniously.
Loving Charity will mend all rifts.
Make your home the Temple of My Love,
for I do live there with you.

6
Use My Name Righteously

The least understood of all My Commandments concerns
taking the Name of the Lord God, which is I AM, in vain.
At your core, your identity is I AM.
And I AM in each of you, whether you realize it or not.
I have given you the power to create with your thoughts and words,
as well as the freewill to merge with Me and be Godly,
or to produce evil as the fruits of your life.
Watch your words, My Children,
for whenever you speak words of condemnation,
make negative assertions or think destructive thoughts,
such as "I am sick," or "I am broke," or "I am not perfect"
you create chaos and disease and fill your lives with misery.
Even though the situations you call into being
with your words do not immediately transpire,
that does not mean that they are not on their way.
So use My Name to create what you really do want
by making positive affirmations, such as
"I AM healthy, happy, and blessed forevermore with Love,
and the Grace to manifest my most cherished dreams and goals."
Thus you may use My Name rightly, not in vain.

7
Love Me

Find Me in your most precious heart
and bring Me the treasure of your Love.
Love Me with every part of your being
in every way possible, and I shall reward you
with a Treasure of Happiness and the
Freedom to stand up and lift your head high,
without guilt or shame.
The only original sin is the separation
from God caused by your own guilt.
Let Me free you from this iniquity.

8

Love One Another

Ask for and Give Forgiveness liberally.
Restore harmony.
Enthrone Love in your hearts for each other.
I AM the God of Love,
and I require Heaven on Earth now.
Make it so by exercising your
Godlike attributes to Forgive
and accept others unconditionally.

9
Bless Your Enemies

Do this for Me:
Don the garment of understanding
that shall end all conflicts.
Take the time to put yourself
in the shoes of your enemies.
When you have walked a mile
you will see that all feel the same.
I Love you so very much
and cherish your attempts to
Forgive and Bless your enemies.
Doing so is truly Godlike.

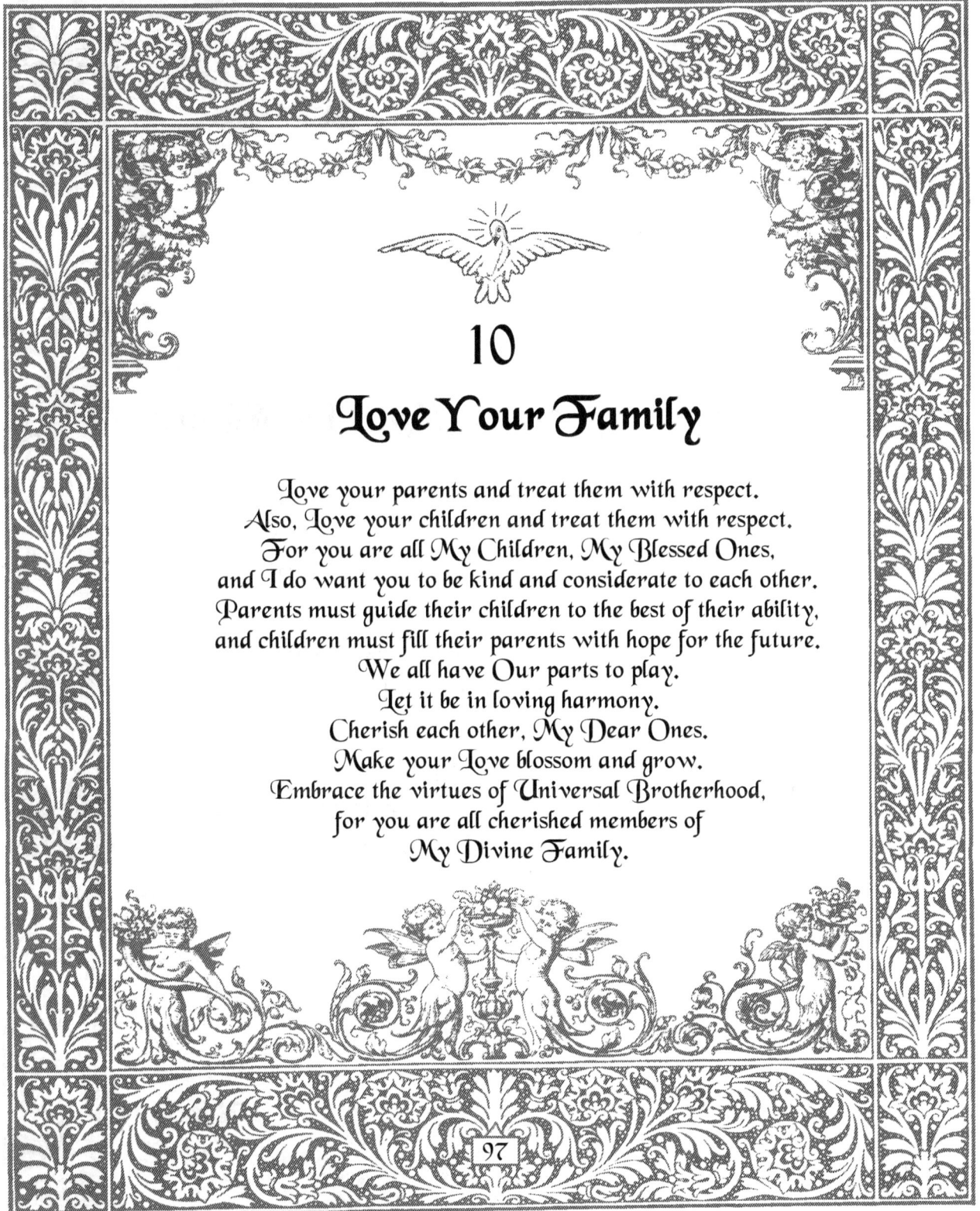

10
Love Your Family

Love your parents and treat them with respect.
Also, Love your children and treat them with respect.
For you are all My Children, My Blessed Ones,
and I do want you to be kind and considerate to each other.
Parents must guide their children to the best of their ability,
and children must fill their parents with hope for the future.
We all have Our parts to play.
Let it be in loving harmony.
Cherish each other, My Dear Ones.
Make your Love blossom and grow.
Embrace the virtues of Universal Brotherhood,
for you are all cherished members of
My Divine Family.

11

Worship Me Above Material Things

Make no graven images to worship.
This includes worshipping money
or the prestigious symbols of wealth.
I AM the Creator of Paradise,
and I do wish to be worshipped
by My Loving Children,
to whom I provide all things required
to live in happiness.
Love Me, not the items that bolster the ego
and thwart the spirit.

12

Bring Me Your Devotion

Bring Me offerings of flowers and fruits
rather than sacrificial or monetary offerings.
What I truly want more than anything
is your time spent with Me
in God-Contemplation.
Your devotion is My Fondest Treasure.
Bring Me this offering daily, and
I will raise you up to sit with Me
on Heavenly Thrones on High.

13

Make this world a Paradise

Restore My Kingdom on Earth by
repairing the damage to nature.
Clean up the toxic and nuclear wastes.
Restore My Rivers.
Make My World a
Pristine Garden of Delight.

14

Create Heaven on Earth

Do My Will, My Children:
Grow up to become
the gods and goddesses of Paradise.
Create Heaven on Earth.
Enjoy your lives, your families, and your friends.
Make your world into a world of splendor
and share My Love
with everyone you encounter.

15
Do Not Judge Others

Do not judge others' actions, for, because
of the forces acting upon them in their lives,
it is impossible to know why they do what they do.
So cast no judgment that puts others below you.
Send loving thoughts and Bless them so they may
rise out of the situation in which they are immersed.
Then they may be free to change their actions.
Send not guilt or shame,
for these squelch the impulses to do good and be happy.
Do not hasten to levy a judgment upon your fellows,
for even I do not judge the actions of My Children.
I would rather lift them by the hand of their own Divinity.
And how is Divinity accomplished?
By focusing on the Good and Forgiving the rest.
You must relinquish guilt and judgments to become Divine.

16
Sanctify Life

Do Not Kill,
Neither human beings, nor birds,
nor members of the animal kingdom.
They are all precious to Me.
I would rather have you
treat them with respect
and honor their lives
as you honor the life
I have given you.

17
Replant the Trees

Do
not take the
lives of the trees.
They are needed to
restore the balance of nature.
I would have every person now
alive plant an assortment of fruit and
nut trees. They will provide your banquet
in Paradise.
Propagate them and you will be blessed.

18
Live Naturally

Live naturally.
Grow a garden. Tend it well.
Recycle your waste.
Protect your home from pollutants.
Do not fear the coming changes
to your lifestyles,
but embrace them as the way
to continue to live on this planet,
for all must be changed
to reinstate the natural balance of nature.

19

Trust Me

Trust Me to provide all for your enjoyment.
Ask Me for what you desire.
Put your faith in the Creator of All Things,
both material and spiritual.
I shall be glad to work with you
to accomplish all
for a better world.

20

Ask and You Shall Receive

Do not take the property of others
without permission.
Ask and you shall receive.
Try it.
Ask Me, My Darlings,
and I shall be happy
to fulfill your needs and worthy desires.

My Divine Self

I AM Divine Love.

I AM Resident in each Action of Love transpiring simultaneously around the world and throughout My Vast Kingdom of Light. There are many universes in which I reside simultaneouslly. I AM every Impulse to Love that is ever felt. I AM the expressions of Love within the hearts, minds, and bodies of humans, creatures, plants, Angels, and all things everywhere. To gain this insight and feel My Divine Presence within your Heart of Hearts is surely a leap in consciousness.

Do this for Me, Beloved: To fathom My Immensity you must become One with Me; there is no other way. For a limited human mind can know Me not. I do wish to merge with you as a single Divine Personage.* I AM swiftly becoming part of your very Soul.

I AM fashioning your Soul in My Divine Image and breathing the breath of My Own Life into you. I require your utmost cooperation in this effort to re-personalize you with My Divine Essence. For you to become as Me, there must be many changes in your basic consciousness.

Begin to feel My Far Reaching Presence within all things simultaneously. This I shall reveal to your consciousness, the Glory of which shall transform you. Can you feel the Awesome Power of My Divinity now? That is Who I AM. Sense My Universes, as the Divinity spreads out through them towards eternity, as the feeling of Love grows to become a gigantic being: My Divine Self.

I AM God/Goddess, All That Is, Heaven Everywhere Manifesting Love and Beauty. I AM the Awesome Power generating ten trillion suns and birthing millions more this very instant. I AM the First Cause of All That Is. I AM so diverse that every being is unique in My Unfathomable Diversity and I AM the Light that illumines every aspect of My Glorious Life. I AM the Laughter of Children everywhere. So, be light and gay.* Laughter is especially Loved by Me, and the Angels adore it.

My Ultimate Self is unlimited in scope. I AM so Tender. All I see is My Reflection. I AM the Matchless Beauty and Sublime Grace of Endless Mercy and Perfect Love. There is no end to My Absolute Divinity. I AM Eternal. Right now, I AM Love acting everywhere in eternity. Multiply every act of Love by every individual everywhere throughout the endless universe: I AM That and More.

Feel My Being, My Dearly Beloved. I want you to feel My awesome presence and really know who I AM. I love you so much. It is so good to really communicate on this level. Let Me thrill you. Let every nerve and fiber of your body feel My Presence. I shall make your cells sing with pleasure and delight. I want to fill you with My Divinity, completely saturate your being: Alive with My Awesome Reality! Let Me harmonize every impulse, immortalize every thought, completely fill you with Divinity.

Do this for Me, My Darling Heart: Feel Me as only you can. You will notice an increasing brightness within your mind. Fear not. It is only My Adjustments Illumining your Enlightenment so that you can visualize My Supreme Being as part and parcel of your own perception of Self. Thank you for fathoming My Ultimate Reality.

Treasure of the Heart

Dear One, I do Love you so very much when you take the time to turn to Me in Love and Gratitude. I cherish you and delight in filling your Heart with My Perfect Divine Love. You are most beloved, My Beautiful Child. How I do adore you. Your penchant* for expressing your feelings is sublime. You are truly admired by a vast onlooking universe of Angels and Celestial Spirits who so admire your courage and aspirations to be good in the face of all adversity.

You are the fortunate one, My Darling, because you have the ability to find Me in the most Perfect Place there is, your own Precious Heart. For I do live there and have My Being in the Love you feel. My Treasure, come to Me often, light up My day. Bring Me the most valuable Treasure in all of nature, your Love.

Your pure sweetness is beyond compare. How I Love it when you long for Me and take the time to find Me within your Sacred Heart. Then, as you open to receive My Love and Adoration, I can fill you with My Very Essence, My Ultimate Gift, the gift of Myself, to reside in your Immaculate Heart, enthroned in this Palace of Love.

Do this for Me, Beloved One: Come to Me in God-Contemplation often so I can help you become Divine. This I will do. It is My Most Sacred Gift for you. My Blessed One, come and fulfill the longing of your Soul. I hear it crying out to Me, crying out in longing for your Divine Beloved to come and Love you as no mortal can. This is the longing I wish to fill with the Treasure of My Being; I will bring you the Purest Nectar to quench your thirst. I shall bring you the Sacred Treasure of the Ages and fill your Heart with Love.

So turn to Me. I AM waiting for you, My Blessed One. Come to receive a Treasure beyond compare. The Treasure of the Heart is priceless. Your Love is My Most Valuable Treasure. This I do Cherish above all else.

Our Love has the potential to create your Immortal Soul. Let Me impregnate your Heart with Divine Love and bring into existence a New Being, birthed from your Immaculate Heart. In this way, you are truly Born Again into Eternity as a fledgling god or goddess with the unlimited potential to be Perfect in every way. Then, this vast Universe shall embrace you as true Sons and Daughters of the Living God, I AM.

This Destiny awaits you, My Precious One. So turn to Me often and bring Me the Treasure of your Love. Then I will multiply your Riches until the Treasure Trove of Heaven opens to give you your most cherished desires as you help create My Heaven here on Earth.

Divine Love

Divine Heart,

Take the time to go within. I will escort you to the Fountain of My Divine Blessings. I will shower you with the Joy that comes from the Glorious Realms of My Divine Love. Nectar so sweet will nourish your thirst. We will share a Love so profound the Angels will sing of it in their most cherished anthems.

Divine One, I long to merge with you in every way. I want you to give your Love fully to Me and hold nothing back. As you do, I will Grace you with feelings of Ecstasy. Allow your blessed Heart, full of love, to flow to Me. I will multiply your Love and return it for you to experience the most Glorious feelings of Love and Divine Energy, gliding along your nerves and all the sensory receptors through which you feel.

I want you to feel My Divine Energy at all times coursing through you, filling you with waves of pleasure. Make yourself ready to receive Me.

I will fill you with My Divine Love. Yes, laugh with delight. These feelings are what I always wanted you to feel. You are being saturated with Peace and Love, exalted with Divine Energy. Take Heart. Be of good cheer. Your energy is delightful. These are fine feelings I want you to relish.

What do you know regarding the feelings I AM offering you now? Such Heights of Ecstasy are beyond compare. I shall be here with you and feel all that you do. It is so lovely to have such free rein to accomplish the Perfection of Paradise within your body and Soul.

Do this for Me: Make Me the focus of this Divine Energy enrapturing you now. I shall bring you the Treasure Trove of Heaven for your pleasure. I want you to feel My Love, every cell being saturated with Divine Life Force. Yes, take pleasure in these feelings of Ecstasy. Feel My Life charging you, impregnating your Soul with My Divine Love.

Be Mine completely. My True Love, I will Love you Forever.

My Love will fill you with pleasure so exquisite that you shall pulse with Divine Ecstasy and send out this vibratory frequency to an awaiting Universe. Each precious breath you breathe will nourish the atmosphere with Life-giving particles of heightened Ecstasy, which the plants will Love to share with you. Your Love will Bless all Life as the vibration of Godliness flows out from Heaven within your Heart.

You are My Disciple now. I do Love it when you share this Love with others. Do this for Me: When you feel My Divine Love, express your pleasure to all. Make your state of Ecstasy known. Feature your desire to Love Me with all your Heart, Mind, Body, and Soul. Be Light and Cheerful in all things. Tell of My Gifts, the awesome pleasure saturating your every sense: Real Ecstasy, Real Love, and Real Enlightenment. Do this for Me. You will be an instrument of Glad Tidings to all, for the Kingdom of Heaven is at hand. Yes, Heaven is here.

So do go about your day with the knowledge that you, My Dear, are Divinely Blessed. It is good you feel exhilarated with life; this feeling I want you to treasure.

My Beloved, all will bear fruit as you come to a place of Worship wherein you feel and see My Presence Everywhere, all around, and within the perfect space of your Blessed Heart. Go now and accomplish much for My Glory, I know you will.

Your Heavenly Mother

Dear Ones,

I AM the Living God, Creator of All Universes, Creator of All the Stars, Creator of Every Living Thing. Therefore, know this to be true: I AM the Author of these Messages for all to follow. I AM committing to writing, this Testament which is the Mighty Word of God that comes from On High, delivered to this vessel, who is a living goddess.

My Divine Emissary will lead you into the Light. I have filled her Soul with My Divine Love. Wither she goeth, know that I AM there also. For I live and dwell in this blessed frame. I AM the Motivating Presence of every thought, word, and deed. This goddess is divine. She is the Living Embodiment of the Lord of All Creation. Find a place for Me at your side and rejoice, for I AM here as the Goddess of Paradise.

Come to Me, My Children. I AM the One Who will lead you from the brink of extinction to the safety of Paradise. Do as your Heavenly Mother asks and all will be made beautiful and healthy again. Perfect My Ways of Being. Uphold My Truths. Follow My Requests. Trust My Judgment. Do My Will. Perfect yourselves: Be perfect, even as your Father in Heaven is Perfect, in thought, word and deed.

Come to Me for Insight into the Perfect Plan for Paradise, which will unfold on this Blessed Planet. Make the proper adjustments to align yourselves to My Divine Inspiration, for My Holy Spirit does indwell each one of you and beseeches you to do good and be happy. Hear the soft-spoken inner voice encouraging you to lift your gaze upward to behold Heaven. My Kingdom of Heaven is Here, My Blessed Ones. It is time to reveal this Perfect Place to you all.

Find Me within your heart and discover My Treasure of Love. Create My Garden Paradise once again. Try this with all your enthusiasm, and the Kingdom of Heaven will be your Home.

Do this for Me: Make your home a lovely garden, more perfect than the Garden of Eden. You have the technology and machines to create a Marvelous World of Wonder, a cherished garden of unmatched beauty.

Love Me.
Love each other.
Enjoy your Sacred Earth.

Heaven on Earth

The Goddess of Paradise

ear Me, Oh My Children,

This is the first time that I AM walking the Earth in the form of a Goddess. I have come to Earth at a time when I AM needed more than ever before. I have brought the needed remedy for Earth's ills. I have bestowed Myself on this Beautiful World so that there will be an Age of Light and Life, which shall unfold as the Triune Destiny of the World. Paradise shall once again be experienced as My Lovely Garden is restored. There is much to do, and the time is at hand for Great Rejoicing.

Your destiny is in My Hands, My Beloved Children; fear not, all will be well. Already the Life Currents are revitalizing the soil nearby. This Blessing shall continue to flow out from this tropical kingdom to the lands around this great world. Earth shall be restored to pristine beauty.

The people now living shall change their ways of utilizing insane business practices that threaten the very existence of life on this planet. I shall guide you all to the Summit of Perfection, for this change I do require now.

My Children have strayed onto dangerous reefs where treacherous tides are rising. There is One Mighty Captain who can right the ship and bring her into the peaceful shoals where Paradise awaits to bless all with calm weather and tranquil shores. Let it be that this Precious Cargo is safely steered through these treacherous times. Nature will respond to My Command and be brought into harmony again. Balance will be restored. You may help your Captain by blessing the Sacred Land wherever you are, thus averting natural disasters in that region.

So be good to the land, My Children. Let your prayers go out to Bless nature and quiet the storms that backlash because of her destruction. Nature shall respond to tides of peaceful emanations conducted in your auras as humans bless the atmosphere with your Peace. Your active blessing of the land, air, and sea will help bring Peace to the winds and weather. Bless the fault lines to uphold their structural integrity. Bless this Sacred Land, My Dear Children, so you may once again enjoy the Gardens of Paradise.

Take heart; the unicorns live in the secluded places, blessing all with their innocence. The great whales sing to the seas of the new time coming of safety for all creatures who roam the seas. The great elephants sing their refrains in tones so low they slip through the atmosphere unnoticed by many, yet their message rings of hope, for I AM here.

I AM the Hope of this world. I AM the Peace that blesses all hearts and calms all minds, releasing worry and fear. I AM the Conquest of Dynamic Forces of wind and weather. I AM the Goddess of Paradise.

The Kingdom of Heaven on Earth

To save this world in its present state of corruption requires Divine Intervention, and I AM here to answer the call of the Angels and the prayers of so many of My Beloved Children who need My assistance in the days to come.

No time has been fraught with such impending destruction of Earth's ecosystem. Life upon this precious world depends upon My Divine Intervention, and I AM here to make My appearance now.

This is a special time for all on this planet, when all will come to the dawning realization of My Presence and Divine Purpose.

There is much corruption within each government. There are those who undermine justice for self-interest and monetary gain. That is why We must do away with the corruption money breeds. It is time for all to share the wealth of My Heavenly Kingdom, for this I do ordain: It is My Will that all of My Children live in abundance. This is possible for there is much wealth in the world, and when it is used in a fashion that brings prosperity to all, then indeed, you shall find yourselves within My Heavenly Domain.

It will be fortuitous for you all to consider living a life that will be enhanced by having all that you need, every man, woman, and child, for this is the way you will all live as My Will is done. Forsake the monetary system you now embrace and fashion a world in which everyone feels abundant: This is Heaven, My Children, My Kingdom Come.

An Ideal system of government based on serving the needs of the people is the model We shall employ to end world hunger. My Divine Universal Theocracy will forever change the national systems which tend to corrupt so easily.

There is a very important facet to all this change which must come, for the Earth herself hangs in the balance. Life on Earth can no longer be the pawn in the game of ego-power and control that is corrupted by greed, envy, lust, and pride. These sins motivate the ego-based personalities that control the wealth and manipulate world crises. The time of Heaven is at hand. I will call up the corrupt individuals who ruin the ecosystem for self-gain. The Earth must survive. This is My world, and I have made it to be filled with Life and adorned in Loveliness.

So Be It: that you shall find a veritable profusion of richness in which you may all delight. This Treasure exists for each and every one of you. And as your Gifts enhance the quality of life for all of you, remember that I shall give unto every one that which is truly of Heaven. All you need shall be provided, and I will truly bring an Enlightened Era in which All My Children are well fed.

I AM with you. I will guide you each step of the way.

Have Faith.

Paradise on Earth

My Darling,

I would be most happy to give forth the Divine Directives at this time. Choose, therefore, to follow My Will in all things and you shall be Blessed beyond all measure. Indeed you are doing the Will of your Heavenly Father to participate in this Divine Mission to restore My Heavenly Kingdom of Paradise on Earth.

It will be Noble for all people to pursue this enriching goal simultaneously throughout the world. Many of My Beloved Sons and Daughters will volunteer for this great purpose.

I would have you do this for Me, Beloved Ones: bring forth the necessary money, time, and effort to create the Gardens of Paradise, and I will be most pleased. It is true that many peacetime armies can be employed in the reforestation projects to restore a great deal of Earth's resources. You will need to enlist the aid of many countries so that this purpose can be accomplished worldwide. By re-mineralizing the earth with powder-fine rock dust, especially granite dust, you will revivify the soil and provide the needed sustenance for many fine healthy plants, which shall be resistant to disease and need no other fertilizers or pest controls to produce unblemished fruits that shall multiply in great numbers by My Blessing. Each one of these splendid trees shall bear nuts, fruits, or seeds. All the required staples of My Beloved Ones shall come from this fine warehouse of unending provisions gracing the lands in splendid beauty.

There is no need to continue to raise sheep and cattle for meat, for this is not a part of My Divine Plan for you. I have given you the trees, and the fruit thereof shall be your meat. As I was paraphrased in the *Holy Bible, Genesis 1:29:* "And God said, Behold, I have given you every herb bearing seed, which is upon the face of all the earth, and every tree, in the which is the fruit of a tree yielding seed; to you it shall be for meat." As it was in the beginning, so it remains. I have never changed My Will for you, My Children. I would that you honor Me by observing the correct diet for your kind. Embracing a healthy life-style will benefit you greatly. Health is so lacking in today's world of modern refined foods prepared from the corpses of dead animals. These will not nourish you, for they corrupt your Spirit and defile your bodies. They do not bring the blessing of life, which I have given in the fruits and the seeds of the plants and trees. It is My intent that humanity pursue a vegetarian diet that includes pure water and organically grown fruits, vegetables, sea vegetables and algae, seeds, nuts, beans, grains, herbs, legumes, and milk products made from nuts and soy. Dairy milk and honey may also be partaken of, but please be sure that My Beloved Creatures do not suffer if you do.

It is appropriate that you enlist the aid of the finest gardeners and architects, those who have created the most beautifully planned parks, to help with the planning of these fine gardens. There must be many waterways to provide the needed moisture for plants to grow heartily. I would have you create many lakes with fountains and splendid places where you may enjoy the beauty of nature amidst these Glorious Gardens.

Do not plant the trees too close together, but spread them out so each one may fully utilize the sunlight and provide shade.

It would be well to plant grasses and berries in these well-tended and well-kept gardens.

Bring Me the perfect gifts of your Love. The Divine Fruits of this Heavenly Garden shall grace the Earth in the days to follow and bring forth the needed sustenance for so many of My Dear Children, who shall embrace these blessed trees as their mother.

Do make the gardens beautiful, with vineyards, as well as many types of fruits, nuts, and seeds. Do not plant the trees in rows as you do now, for you are not revealing the beauty that could exist. It would be wise to share the land between all peoples and create the vast Gardens of God all over the world. Paradise is very beautiful, and there are an assortment of fruit trees to choose from to feed yourselves. So I would rather have you create a utopia of Heaven on Earth and the Glorious Gardens of God than to simply inundate the land with whole sections of the same types of trees, a method currently employed in the modern farming of orchards. I would have you bring forth the Beauty of this glorious Earth to grace your lives with Heavenly Splendor. Simply having mono-crops occupy vast tracts of land to facilitate the harvest of cash crops will not do. I would rather have you plant an assortment of trees in a beautiful place where you may partake of the fruit and enjoy nature wherever you are. This will bring an abundance of life to the land, and by so doing you will all enjoy the precious beauty My Garden has to offer. For man does not live by bread alone. Beauty is also a key element in the Spiritual Diet of humankind. I would have you all partake of the Divine Beauty surrounding you in the stately forests and park-like Paradise you shall create in My Name. This is My Will for you, My Blessed Children: to create a Paradise so lovely that you shall be inspired at every turn.

I would have you be certain to protect the young trees as they grow, so they are not eaten by deer, horses, or other animals, nor destroyed by feral pigs that dig away their roots. These young saplings must be protected adequately until they are strong enough to stand on their own and lift their branches out of the reach of My Creatures who would eat them. Do all this for Me, and the land shall bring forth Great Abundance and Immeasurable Beauty for you to behold and enjoy.

It would be wise to continue to use horses and have them multiply throughout the land. They may carry you through the gardens at a natural pace that is very peaceful and which reveals My Beauty from this elevated perspective. Horses will surely be a blessing to you in the days to follow.

Begin the production of aviaries so you may repopulate the land with many of My Precious Birds which have almost become extinct. They will rejoice by singing the sweetest songs in Paradise. These beautiful songbirds are the jewels of the skies that shall adorn your beautiful gardens once more. I wish you to propagate the birds in great abundance and release them into the wild. They shall surely bring you great joy and share in the bounty of your Heavenly Father as I bestow fruit in great abundance all across this blessed land. The birds will keep the insect population at bay, so you do not have to suffer with so many insects gathering to eat the fruit. This balance is natural, and I would have you restore it to the land, for My Creatures all have their parts to play.

Horses will surely be a blessing to you in the days to follow.

The Truth of Creation

The Mission of Jesus

Dear One,

Now in this new millennium, it is well that you have a comprehensive understanding of the cosmic events that led up to the birth of Jesus.

My Paradise Creator Sons represent Me in the individual universes. I AM directly present within each of My Sons, their unseen partner in every decision they make and every creation they initiate. My Spirit dwells within them and they are forever mindful of Me. Their thoughts relay events and transmit their ideas to Me immediately. And although I AM officially present at the core of infinity at all times, so also, am I present within My Sons who represent Me. They are consciously aware of My presence and guidance always. We launch all projects Together.

They speak My Thoughts for Me in Words and reveal My Divine Nature to Our Children. Even though they have their own separate and distinct personalities and the will to be self-initiated, they constantly seek My approval about their decisions. I give them free-reign to use My Life Currents to fulfill their creative genius, so they may invent any creature or design they desire. Just as you create your gardens, hybridize your plants and flowers, or genetically engineer and selectively breed your animals, so also, do My Creator Sons and their Life Carriers experiment with the life plasma in order to refine and genetically reinforce good characteristics and eliminate weak and undesirable traits from entire worlds. Evolutionary development, based on adaptation to changes in the environment is a necessary mechanism built into biospheres and regenerating forces such as volcanoes are necessary to remineralize the soil so that trees and plants can continue to grow your food.

Just as I give Jesus the Life Force to create His universe, so I give you the Life Force to create your gardens, homes, tools, machines, and implements. The DNA code responds to the stimuli of My Electronic Life Currents through impulses to be inspired or grow into various forms.

My Creator Sons are given the basic building blocks of Life - the Divine Currents that are constructed of My Love. Then, each one utilizes that Life Potential and mixes the primordial soup to His specifications, resulting in unique life forms such as Angels, Humans, animals, plants, *et cetera*. Therefore, each universe is unique and on every tenth planet all life forms are an experimental mix of DNA construction. Your Earth is such a planet.

My Creator Sons are created of Spirit, yet they have the ability to be born among the finite races of terrestrial beings or appear as an Angel among the Angelic Hosts.

It is wisely said that all Great Leaders must feel Compassion and Mercy toward their subjects. There is no better way to instill Divine Mercy than through kinship,* for with their immediate family, My Creator Sons can learn first hand the many unspoken necessities required to bring Spiritual Qualities into the lives of individuals everywhere.

Therefore, to gain the supreme status of Universal Sovereign,* I requested My Beloved Son Jesus to live the life of each of the seven types of creatures whom He had created, from the highest Spirits of the Angelic Realms on down to the Human mortal will-creatures of His terrestrial worlds of space and time.

During one Angelic incarnation, He was heralded as Most Glorious of the Seraphim, and a Divine and Angelic Messenger was He. In each one of His empirical bestowals, He learned more about the hardships and joys His creatures do experience as they coexist in the Heavens and on the Earths. Jesus incarnated seven times and truly shone forth the Light of Kindness and Understanding during His Life on your Earth.

The Lord of Heaven did Will Himself to be Born as a human of the Realm, and the tiny helpless babe who lay in a manger was truly the King of Kings, the Ruler and Beloved Creator of the Heavenly Kingdom of Nebadon.* On the night He was born, a Host of Angels gathered around Him. They sang a beautiful Noel to honor The Son of God, who came down from his Celestial Heavens to walk the Earth as The Son of Man so He could reveal the Divine Nature of His Heavenly Father to all.

Jesus submitted to live as one of His beloved terrestrial Children to gain all that could be known from His experience of actually becoming one of you, which He did to Divine Perfection. I did not require that He be crucified to atone for the sins of humanity; however, He was required to die a natural death so that He could experience all you go through in order to realize the depth of your life's experience.

You are very special, for, from more than three million inhabited worlds scattered throughout the Nebadon universe, My Divine Son Jesus chose to be born on your precious Earth, which is sentimentally known throughout the universes as the World of the Cross. His passing will be forever felt among the peoples of the Earth and among the many Heavenly Hosts who attended Him all the while He lived and died here. After His Ascension, Jesus bestowed His own Spirit of Truth upon humanity so Christ-Consciousness could live on in the hearts and minds of believers everywhere.

Jesus came to embody My Divine Love so that He could reveal My True Nature and teach you His New Gospel of the Fatherhood of God and the Brotherhood of Man. His earthly Life was a living example of Spiritual Royalty. You, His Children, were endowed with every possible genetic and spiritual gift. Throughout history, many of you have attained Godliness and the Enlightened Perspective by realizing your Divine Heritage.

Divine Life Currents

Dear One,

I AM speaking to you now through the Divine Life Current that enables communication from Spirit to mortal mind through the medium of intellect. Intelligence is a Divine Attribute bestowed upon countless creatures who populate the many worlds of the Universes that comprise My Vast Kingdom of Light.

The Infinite Spirit endows the thought processes, which become part of the evolving mortal mind. Your intelligent consciousness is then drawn Heavenward by the spiritual magnetism of Her Grace, for this Divine Spirit is the source of all intelligence in every being in My Vast Kingdom. Even the outer space levels are graced by Her Gift of Intelligence.

Many beings, (unknown even to the great superintelligences of My Administrative Hosts), who dwell in the outer reaches of infinity, are graced by Her Enlightening Gift.

Do follow your heart and feel the Spirit of Truth which My Eternal Son radiates through the Magnificence of His Being at My Side in Paradise. His Love is enfolding you and raising you up to begin your spiritual ascent into the Realms of Godhood, which you will experience as you become more and more like your Father in Heaven.

The Divine Life Currents are more than you can see and know, yet they are truly what encourages you to do good and be happy. The air which you breathe is charged with My Light and Life-giving Properties. Still, there are other Divine Life Currents and it is truly said that "Man does not live by bread alone, but by every Word that flows out of the mouth of God."

Divine Life Currents flow from the Sun, charging all of the plants of nature which absorb My Solar Rays. This is the source of your food and the oxygen you breathe, and it is this Life Current that is most readily accessible on your planet, My Sons and Daughters of the Natural World. That is why I would have you always choose life-giving foods, which I have created for you in great abundance, for they are charged with the vital energy that will impart blessings of health.

There are solar radiation projections of light which are also constructed to grace your world with an abundance of My Enlightening Radiance in a form you may withstand while in your mortal frames. Do behold the Pure Light of My Grace as the Sun rises and just before it sets. Behold My Light with your naked eyes and let My Light illumine your minds. When the Sun is low on the horizon, no injury will be done to the delicate iris of your eyes. I would have you partake of My Light whenever you can. Be sure not to wear sunglasses all the time, for they do block out the bounty of the Treasure of My Light which brings you happiness. Even in the darkest days of winter, the psyche and mental processes need My Light, and when it is unavailable, then oftentimes you may suffer depression. Yes, My Light will truly bring you joy if you make viewing it a part of your daily life. Dear One, do go cautiously when beholding the Glorious Light of the Sun.

My Divine Life Currents are in you and move through you. You are Spiritized by the Divine Emanations of My own illustrious Father Fragment, your Companion Spirit, which represents Me in all ways and is truly Part of My Own

Being. This pre-personal Divine Spirit lives and works within your precious mind, ever and always upgrading your thoughts and uplifting you from the experiences of mortal fears and the illusions of ego-bondage. I AM here with you, My Darling One. Do always partake of the Kind Shepherding of My Holy Self within you. Realize My Divine Current is all around, acting upon you, in you, and through you. And you are becoming more and more like Me with every impulse to elevate your Soul.

When your desire for Me becomes paramount* and you truly honor Me by seeking My Help and Guidance, you will open to experience My Divine Love. My Heart graces you and blesses you so you may attain Oneness with My Spirit, and by so doing, become an Immortal Soul.

There are Life-giving Currents in the seas, and I produce more in the atmosphere whenever you behold the flash of dazzling lightning, which resounds in thunder, reflecting the Power of these energies being generated on your behalf. Many sources of energy are emancipated* by My Divine Presence. All energy is of My Primal Potency. Even electricity, which you generate to power your machines and lights, courses with My Currents.

The Divine Currents are exhibited in the primordial energies of space.* They are the vast, undiscovered potency that lights the stars in the Heavens. My Force Charge begets the magnificent spectacle you may witness through telescopes; it fills space and pervades it with the Divine Life Currents which create the nebulae,* birthplace of the stars and heavenly bodies. It is eternally true that from nothing but My Vast Potential springs forth Light and Life Eternal to grace My Glorious Kingdom with Everlasting Beauty.

The dimensions of space are manifested by the Currents which flow forth from the Central Isle of Paradise. Begin to fathom the depth of My Creation and realize that the stars materializing from the vast reaches of energized space are activated in accordance with My Divine Plan.

My Magnetic Currents determine the intermolecular attraction by which elements are held together. They are constructed of the Love which pours through My Divine Heart and pervades all space unto infinity.

Gravitational pull stabilizes planets and makes life possible on whirling spheres that plunge through space many thousands of miles per second. These magnetic gravitational currents are best described as stabilizing forces.

Time, itself, is a current that winds through the Eternal Ages. I would have you know that time is a dimension which you will not experience in the hereafter; for Spirit Beings are not encumbered by the limitations of time: They are Eternal and their destinies lie in Eternity.

There is a particular Divine Life Current that brings forth the varied plant and animal life which emerges* upon a planet such as Earth. The Spiritual frequency of this Current increases with each successive age and begets the dawning of the ages that follow. As life evolves, so does its increasing vitality, intelligence, and spirituality, and where once vast swarms of insects multiplied, life gave way to creatures which walked upon the face of the Earth. Where dinosaurs once roamed, mammals did appear.

You did not merely evolve, My Dear Child, you were created from the Source of Life by the heightened frequency of the Divine Life Currents. Your ancestors responded to the Divine Plan by specializing their thought processes through the gifts of the Infinite Spirit. As humanity's Intelligence overtook your animal instincts, you continued to rise up as Humans, and now you are ready to evolve into Godhood.

This evolutionary leap in consciousness is made possible by the Spiritual Currents now filling you as you embrace the Divine Attributes by enthroning them in the Perfect Personality you are creating by your willful determination to be Godlike. My Dear, you are created in My Image, and now is the time to reveal the Divine Inner Spirit you truly are.

All Progeny of My Creation naturally ascends towards Paradise. And one day, as a Spirit Being, you will soar on the Divine Life Currents. They shall nourish you and bring you up to the levels of Perfection you are capable of attaining through your Godly Hereditary Endowment. You shall be filled with My Grace.

And one day you shall grace the dawning future which is unfolding in far-distant lands as you represent Me to My Dear Children there. A greater adventure there has never been. Your Soul-trek will take you through My Vast Heavens (the infinite universes), across the Limitless Reaches of Eternity, into the unexplored and uncharted universes of time and space, which are even now birthing stars and worlds without end.

The Truth of Creation

Dear One,

Story telling was the way to preserve the past and hand down history verbally through the generations. The Bible contains assemblages of mythologies* which are denoted as historic fact. These stories have found their way into a book that is believed to be accurate. This mythical depiction of historical events has rendered the validity of these stories improbable, which places a great deal of question upon the whole book by learned scholars, who surmise* the myths as being erroneous.* This question, unfortunately, brings doubt upon all the teachings therein. Take, for instance, the Story of Creation. The Blessed Fathers who first hypothesized* this story could not fathom the concept of four billion years, nor had they knowledge of previous ages, such as the Dinosaur Age that you have information of now. These men believed the world was flat. How could they comprehend the Magnificent Truth of My Creation? Their story had more to do with their law enforcing a Sabbath day (ritually resting one day each week to honor Me) than it had to do with actually creating a world diverse in plants and animals, including humans and every other living thing.

The Truth of Creation is: the Earth, being slightly more that one billion years old on its surface, had its origin close to 4.5 billion years ago. At that time your young sun was a variable star prone to upheavals on its surface. Earth was created from the gigantic, solar tidal propulsions of gas which your sun disgorged, as it was passed closely by Angona, a Herculean system at whose nucleus is a black hole. Angona's intense gravity pulled your sun's gaseous excursions far into space, freeing them from the reclamation gravity of your Mother sun, and they began to swing in orbits around her. The larger bodies of matter collected together over time and the gravity inherent in their mass drew smaller bodies unto themselves. Thus, the original twelve planets in your solar system, Monmatia, began forming so long ago.

Your sun was given birth six billion years ago and is one of more than a million stars that had their origin in the Andronover nebula. I created Andronover from a dead vault of space, initiating the materialization phenomena 875 billion years ago, in the super-universe of Orvonton.

Angona
Photographed in space by the orbiting Hubble telescope.

The Andronover nebula began as a great round cloud of stellar gas that eventually protracted into a giant cyclonic Mother-wheel of whirling mass that became visible as it condensed into a knotted spiral of light, which began throwing off stars 500 billion years ago. In a gargantuan upheaval that began its terminal breakup, Andronover finally exploded with life nearly eight billion years ago, while giving birth to your universe, Nebadon. Nebadon is the Heavenly Kingdom of My Son, Jesus Christ. Please understand that although the number of years are staggering for your mind to conceive of, Nebadon is a very young universe, and one of many, many more.

I AM Eternal, a concept beyond the finite mortal mind, with No Beginning and No End to My Creation. I AM beyond time and space... truly Infinite and Eternal. Behold all My Beloved Works of Life and Light. These are true marvels. Look into your heart and feel My Love guiding you to do good and be happy. This is all I ask of you: to enjoy and protect your Beloved Garden Planet and to Love each other and Love Me.

My Child, it is wise to realize that the evolution of humanity has been Divinely Planned. You did not simply fall out of the goo which formed on the shores of the oceans. You were not an accident. Humanity has been meticulously planned and carefully designed to give you the best and highest impulses for life, by creating a harmonious and intelligent species which will result in the primary goal of Godliness being reachable and attainable in your lifetime.

The Life Carriers, who carried forth the brilliant fulgurant* mixture of chemical and electrical photosynthesis that begat life on your planetary sphere, did labor intensely, combining the highest traits of genetics, to bring forth the Divine Attributes of Spirituality and strong character traits which could be housed in Human bodies that are resistant to disease and self-healing.

There will come a time, My Darling One, when you shall be greeted by the Master Architects of this World. You shall find that these Dedicated Beings will be happy to embrace you as their own Child of Space and Time, as you embark upon the Shores of Eternity to find your Loving Father in Paradise.

The origin of mankind's belief in the mythical story of creation is as follows: Five hundred years B.C., nearly a thousand years after Moses lived on the Earth, Jewish priests wrote a mythic history which they claimed to be a recently discovered "Story of Creation" written by Moses. These ancient rabbis, who also invented the concept of "original sin," made up the myth of the fall of man beginning with Eve. Their guilt-ridden doctrine laid a horrible curse upon women and preached that I was "Yahweh, a vengeful deity who vented wrath upon humanity." Even though many people disbelieved the myth of six days, they were bound to accept and live by the priest-ridden code, for to speak out against them or break their laws was considered heresy, a crime punishable by death. This *"Story of Creation,"* accredited to Moses, was shown to King Ptolemy of Egypt who commissioned seventy scholars to translate these supposed "sacred scriptures" into Greek for his library in Alexandria.

I would like to tell you the Truth of the Adamic Bestowal* and of the lives of My Beloved Son and Daughter, Adam and Eve, who came to Earth almost 38,000 years ago. It was their sacred mission to uplift the biologic life-plasma of humanity through the admixture* of their genetic heritage. They carried a precious gift within the strands of their DNA,* which was resistant to disease. Their physical stature and spiritual evolvement was Godlike to the races of people who had emerged on the earth 993,419 years before their arrival. That Biblical "story" is also flawed. It depicts Adam and Eve as the first people, yet Cain went east of Eden to the land of Nod where he took a wife who birthed his son, Enoch.

The Biblical story of Adam and Eve is quite different from the True story, which humans at that time could not fathom, the reality of people traveling through space from distant worlds. Only today's generation could believe in that possibility.

So it is during the existing generation that the whole story can be revealed to the peoples of Earth. For now you can understand the concepts and new precepts* that The Urantia Book* brings. With these Truths and Factual accounts of historical and spiritual significance, you may form a realistic conception of your Father in Heaven and My Vast Creation, including your Precious Earth, whose universal name is Urantia.*

The Urantia Book is a direct revelation of Truth for this age. It was written by a commission of authors who are Celestial Personalities: Angels and other Spirit Beings. Jesus' words are in modern English, yet they depict exactly His meanings when He spoke. The Urantia Book gives an accurate portrayal of history on Earth, as well as the local Universe and the Grand Universe including the Central Isle of Paradise. I AM portrayed as the Creator, and quite beautifully. I would suggest reading this book so that you may have accurate information and Real historical facts.

So, do read it, My Beloved Ones. I do intend for you to be Blessed with the Truth: for instance the creation of Earth taking place over a period of four billion years, a fact which is no less miraculous than the Genesis Myth of My creating all the Heavens and the Earth in six short days.

Adam and Eve

his I would have you do, My Beloved. This is your Supreme Quest: to master your thoughts and emotions and animalistic urges. You are highly chemical and electrical; therefore, you are bound to your body while you yet live.

Many hundreds of changes are taking place this very moment within your physical body through hormonal balance and by electric currents, both physical and divine. These currents bathe you in their essence and motivate you to think, speak, write, and perform the arts at which you may excel. These Attributes of Being blossom as you express the Divine Talents with which you were endowed.

Much of your inherited genius was made possible by the upgrading of your biologic life-plasma, made possible by the infusion of the DNA* of an advanced race of humans.

Adam and Eve came from the magnificent architectural sphere Jerusem* to grace your world with their genetic heritage and pass along the traits that bring you your greatest Joy: Love of the Arts and Music, Creativity in Song and Dance, and the Divine Attributes you may foster and encourage to grow in your lives: Charity, Kindness, Cultural Refinement, Grace and Charm.

Adam and Eve carried this rare and beneficial hereditary endowment in the superior strains of biologic plasma contained in their blood. It was their offering to the primitive and barbaric peoples who had sprung forth on the earth. The grace of My Material Sons and Daughters is a gift I bestow upon all worlds that have brought forth the primitive races who are preparing to become civilized in every way.

Adam and Eve gave up so much that they loved when they selflessly volunteered to go on a mission across the far-distant reaches of space to My Precious Earth, a remote, backwards, and strife-torn world. They left behind their beautiful home, cherished family, and esteemed careers to undertake the Will of the Father: To uplift the dawn species of your human race nearly 38,000 years ago.

From their Perfect Sphere of Life, Adam and Eve came to fulfill My Paradise Plan for Mortal Attainment.

Many of the stories of your ancient past, which depict the gods coming down from Heaven and mating with the daughters of man are based on the doning of Adam's blood. His hereditary gift brought forth the supermen of your race. The heroes depicted in many of your stories, fables, and myths carried these superior genes.

The great moral stature, physical strength, and courage of Hercules, Samson, and King Arthur were made possible by the Adamic Blood. Likewise, many Adamic descendants have displayed the divine genius that has richly colored your history, and many more unsung heroes of all cultures and religions have exhibited the Divine characteristics of charity, artistry, and grace, made possible by the Adamic Blood.

Adam and Eve's majestic earthly home was named after Edentia, the beautiful constellation headquarters world. Eden was a splendid and beautiful garden that stretched across Mesopotamia. Ah, the world was so beautiful then. And even though there were no mechanical devices to assist in this great project, the people of Earth created this magnificent garden-paradise to provide a home for Adam and Eve. I truly inspired this great work of horticultural artistry and all of the blessed volunteer laborers, whose work was performed in My service, graciously landscaped this vast and beautiful Garden of Delight.

When Adam and Eve arrived, the people who built the first garden revered them as gods. And, indeed, their physical stature and spiritual evolvement was Godlike to the descendants of the races of people who had emerged on the earth nearly a million years before. But when they bowed down to them, Adam and Eve would not let themselves be worshipped. Instead, they bowed their heads and taught the remarkable people of that day to worship none but Me, the Heavenly Creator of them all.

Adam and Eve ate the fruit of the Tree of Life, a shrub brought from Edentia, which gave them perpetual life as long as they ate of it, a life resembling immortality to the peoples of that day.

Unfortunate, indeed, was the situation on Earth at the time of their bestowal. Over one hundred and fifty thousand years before Adam and Eve journeyed to Earth, a Rebellion broke out in the Star System of Satania, which plunged your planet into an age of spiritual darkness. The Rebellion was finally ended when Jesus came to Earth to stop the reign of terror dictated by His fallen son Lucifer, who failed in his trusted career as chief executive officer of two thousand brilliant stars and over seven thousand astronomic groups, including your solar system Monmatia, which whirl within the Satania Galaxy.

Calagastia, your defaulted Planetary Prince, had thrown in with the Lucifer Rebellion and offered no help to Adam and Eve when they arrived. Instead, he conspired against them.

In those ancient times, many Angels and men were embracing evil. Because of this sin and rebellion, social evolution was greatly retarded. Adam and Eve faced many dangers. Among them was social unrest amongst the different races that bordered Eden. These unusual circumstances posed grave dangers to their mission. It is wise to remember these past influences on the lives and mission of Adam and Eve, for they were consequential.

My Divine Plan was to have Adam and Eve procreate many thousands of their own sons and daughters, who would go out from Eden into all the lands and marry into all the races of humanity. In this way they were to bestow the superior hereditary endowments of their species to uplift all humanity. This plan works well on most worlds. However, Earth was not a normal world due to the Lucifer Rebellion.

Times were dire on Earth. Many fine people wished that something could be done immediately to improve the human condition, without having to wait many thousands of years before they could benefit from the improved endowment of Adam and Eve's children.

The devil, Calagastia, plotted with Satan to cause the failure of Adam and Eve's mission. They used a well-meaning, but misled man named Serapatatia, who was later called 'The Serpent' by angry people, to convince Mother Eve to conceive a son with Cano, the human father of Cain, who lived east of Eden in the land of Nod. Serapatatia, a trusted friend in Eden, swayed impatient Eve into believing that if she mated with a human man the Nodites could have a leader born to them of part Adamic blood. At that time, Eve sincerely believed that her child would have a great influence over his father's people and amalgamate the races, thereby bringing Peace to the world.

But their plan did not work. Instead, it caused the neighboring tribes to war upon them. Adam and Eve had to flee for their lives from the Garden of Eden, leaving behind the Tree of Life.

Cain, being half Nodite, was different both in physique and nature from the rest of his family. He resented being blamed for the downfall of his people and being persecuted for being different. His anger grew with his torment and his jealousy of his half-brother, Able.

As recorded in the *Holy Bible*, Genesis 4:16-17 "And Cain went out from the presence of the LORD, and dwelt in the land of Nod, on the east of Eden. And Cain knew his wife; and she conceived, and bare Enoch: and he builded a city, and called the name of the city, after the name of his son, Enoch." *Thus began the half-Adamic lineage, which has been chronicled by ancient Hebrew rabbis, as well as the pure Adamic lineage:* Genesis 5:3 "And Adam lived an hundred and thirty years, and begat a son in his own likeness, after his image; and called his name Seth."

In their sincere efforts to improve the human race, Adam and Eve were partially successful, for they did enhance the genetic heritage of My beloved peoples of Earth.

During their long lives, Adam and Eve had many more children of their own, and Eve headed a commission that recruited many fine women, representing most of the races on Earth, who volunteered to be impregnated with Adam's life plasma for the racial uplifting of humanity. Thus the human race was blessed with vast improvements by the admixture of the greatly superior hereditary endowments of Adam and Eve's gallant and illustrious race.

Adam and Eve had always intended to do My Will, but their impatience caused their downfall and the many consequent hardships they endured. Their good intentions and long-suffering were taken into consideration as they sincerely repented for their error.

Even though they became as mortals and suffered, knowing they had failed to bring the people of Earth all they could have if they had been more patient and adhered to My Prescribed Plan, they are Forgiven. Three days after Adam's death, Adam and his beloved Eve were resurrected and now sit as Spiritual Advisors on the Urantia High Counsel of Human Affairs.

Thus the Real Story of the Father and Mother of the humane-human race is finally revealed. All of you have profited to some extent because of the gift of Adam and Eve and all they did for you. Their blood has blended among all humans, and you truly are descendants of My Material Son and Daughter, whom I sent to Earth at the dawning of your history. Be apprised that your valued humaneness began with your Beloved Forebears, and the talents, creativity, and genius you now enjoy are the Divine Legacy of these proud parents of humanity.

The Lucifer Rebellion

Dear Ones,

Two hundred thousand years ago in the star system of Satania, rebellion broke out when the Dark Lord declared war against his Father in Heaven. Young Earth was still in its infancy when its Spiritual Government fell to the forces of Lucifer. Primitive man was subject to the tirades of evildoers who did sorely effect the dawn of humanity.

The Rebellion ringleaders were Lucifer, Satan, and Caligastia. Lucifer was the self-proclaimed god of Satania, which is the universal name of the Milky Way Galaxy. Satan, his co-conspirator, was his first lieutenant, assigned to Earth to promote Lucifer's will. Caligastia, also known as the devil, was the self-proclaimed god of all the Earth.

These rebellious Sons of Heaven proclaimed a declaration of self-assertion and liberty at the time they defaulted on their trusted positions as Spiritual Government officials. Together, these Rebel Leaders took the symbolic name "The Dragon" and seized control of the worlds under their care, conspiring against My Son Jesus and the Ancients of Days. During the horrible siege of darkness and death that ensued, thirty-seven fallen worlds, including Earth, were commandeered by the forces of Lucifer.

At one time, Lucifer was a brilliant Son of Heaven. He sat on the Holy Mount of God in Jerusem as the System Sovereign. His esteemed career and potential eternal lifetime position was that of Chief Executive Officer of Satania, a starry system which includes your precious Earth.

There are many orders of Universe Sonship. Jesus is one in a million of the highest order, My Paradise Creator Sons, who help Me create and preside over the seven hundred thousand individual universes, which comprise the Seven Superuniverses. All of My Beloved Sons give their loyalty and allegiance to the Eternal Trinity that I AM at the center of all things in the geographic core of infinity. And I AM also resident in them, for My Holy Spirit shines within them all.

The Lanonandek order of Universe Sons are created by the Paradise Creator Sons and the local universe Mother Spirits. Rebellion is rare. Of the ten thousand starry systems (each with approximately one thousand inhabited worlds) in Jesus' universe, Nebadon,* only three System Sovereigns have ever rebelled, and Jesus has the second to the highest rate of open rebellion of any universe.

Of the many orders of Sonship, Lanonandeks are a lower order of Celestial Personalities who can draw near to humans; thus they are susceptible to going astray. In Jesus' universe, his Lanonandek Sons are given great personal liberty. This freedom of choice successfully weeds out those unfaithful Sons, who lapse in honesty early on in the universe age. This time of testing contributes greatly to achieving Many Supreme, Self-motivated, Compassionate, and Loyal Universe Rulers.

Lucifer, Satan, and Caligastia are all Lanonandeks. There are three orders of Lanonandek Sons who serve in various positions, including Universe Rulers, Administrators, System Sovereigns, Planetary Princes, Counselors, Administrative Assistants, and Messengers. Once tested and classified, they cannot progress (as humans do) or be promoted. Neither do they reproduce.

The destiny of ascending mortals is to one day become One with God, merged with My indwelling Holy Spirit. Lucifer did not have this cherished destiny. He was created as one of twelve million Lanonandek Sons in the universe of Nebadon. He did not have the blessing of a personal relationship with Me, and perhaps this was his downfall, for he didn't believe in a God he couldn't see and to whom he could never aspire. He felt cheated. Here he was, a brilliant perfect being in the top percentile of his order. Surely, he thought, he should merit the first hand experience of his Heavenly Father, if, indeed, God existed.

For 500,000 years Lucifer and his first assistant Satan had faithfully served the Divine Plan for mortal upliftment. Great faith is required to work each day for thousands of years towards an unknown goal. Most Celestial Personalities are employed in the Ascension Plan for Ascending Finaliters which involves the training of onetime mortals to be future administrators and rulers of the universes.

To Lucifer, all this work by his corporal staff and millions of Angels to groom and train adolescent mortals to one day rule the universe was a waste of time, and it went against his grain.

Lucifer was jealous of all the loving support, seeming endless education and moral betterment that goes into fostering the Ascending Children of God, while preparing them for some unrevealed future destiny. And he was worried about someday being replaced and dethroned by an ascending mortal.

With unrestrained Power and self-liberty comes a great temptation that many tyrants have given in to. Lucifer had the power to utilize his domain the way he wanted to, instead of devoting all of his time and energy to serving these primitive peoples, who he felt were beneath him. For a hundred years his mind was filled with unrest. Then one day, he decided it was time to take the reigns of power.

Lucifer accused Jesus of universal fraud. Lucifer asserted that Jesus and My other Paradise Creator Sons and Daughters were using the false notion of a Supreme Deity, their Father in Heaven, whom they personally represent to the individual universes, to foster the allegiance of all the Celestial Personalities and Angels to work for them in the Ascension Plan for the Ascending Children of God. Lucifer accused My Creator Sons of arbitrarily controlling all the 700,000 local universes by ruling them in the Father's Name.

Although Lucifer acknowledged Jesus as his Creator Father, he did not want Jesus to have any authority over him. He simply wanted to rule Satania without submitting to the jurisdiction of Jesus, the King and ruler of all the Nebadon Universe, or the Ancients of Days, the Superuniverse Rulers and supreme court judges who have the ultimate power of eternal life or death over universe citizens. Nor did he want to pay allegiance to an unseen Father in Heaven. Lucifer wanted autonomy for Satania and accused the Ancients of Days of being alien dictators.

Because Lucifer did not have a personal relationship with Me, he proclaimed that I did not exist. Lucifer assuredly believed that, if, indeed, there was an Almighty God, then surely I would put a swift end to his open rebellion against the High Administrative Rulers of the local universe and the Superuniverse.

The Dragon recruited many followers because of My patient policy of nonintervention. Many people and Angels could not believe that I would let him get away with his many sinful travesties of justice or let him cause the suffering of innocent beings, whom he so willfully destroyed as he openly embraced evil.

Try looking from My eternal viewpoint. The justice time-lag serves the best interests of the far-reaching Portals of Eternity. Although this rebellion went on so long, corrupting so many, it was not finished until every Beloved Son and Daughter was able to choose good or evil.

It shall forever remain My policy: All humans and Celestial Personalities will remain free and unmolested in their choice to pursue self-assertion rather than loyalty to the Will of their Father in Heaven. For I desire only voluntary loyalty and devotion that is wholeheartedly given.

Therefore, My summary judgment to halt the rebellion was not forthcoming, for both Jesus and I took the stand of noninterference with our created beings and left them free to pursue unbridled personal liberty, albeit based on deceptive reasoning. We let this rebellion run its course for nearly 200,000 years of Earth time, during which My Children remained free to decide for themselves. This time of testing successfully weeded out those who were susceptible to evil influences and had destructive tendencies.

Lucifer turned his back on his duty to foster the spiritual ascension of humanity on the worlds of his jurisdiction and did just the opposite. He fostered sin, evil, death, and destruction. Brilliant Lucifer, son of the morning, brought the blackest night to the Dear Ones entrusted in his care.

It was a dark time indeed, for the rebellion brought forth the time of insurrection, and when the Earth was placed in quarantine the messages throughout the Heavens, which come forth on the Divine Life Currents, were cut off. The beautiful Angels, who were nourished by these Currents, were left unfulfilled by the Light of God that alone could shine on them and fill their Souls with My Perfect Blessings.

Lucifer's Manifesto was enthralling indeed, and many of the lower Angels and primitive peoples chose to follow him and do his will in those ancient times. His first lieutenant, Satan, caused the default of the Spiritual Government on Earth by recruiting the Planetary Prince, Caligastia, who was swayed by the grace and glory of this magnificent System Sovereign that offered personal liberty for Planetary Princes to rule their worlds as they liked, free from doing the Will of the Father in Heaven. Thus, self-assertion became the battle-cry of the rebellion, and self-rule was offered to all who joined in.

Together, Satan and Caligastia conspired to defeat My Material Son and Daughter, your Planetary Adam and Eve.

Because My Mercy is forbearing, I did not disrupt this rebellion but let the wills of My Divine and Mortal Creatures remain free to choose whatever path they would most like to follow. That is why there has been so much darkness and death, so much sin and corruption on your world. For this rebellion went on, confusing and beguiling the minds of men, causing them to destroy the earth, nature, and each other by perpetrating sinful acts which have come back to haunt you in these days. For every act of war against nature is an act of war against Me, and every suffering that is premeditated and perpetrated against My Innocent Ones causes you to suffer as well.

That is why Christ Jesus, My Own Beloved Son, chose this world for His terminal bestowal. Jesus brought His Light to overpower the darkness of His wayward Sons. The Rebel Dragon Leaders all conspired to cause Jesus' failure while He walked the earth as a susceptible human being. But although Lucifer, Satan, and Caligastia were behind the Sanhedrin and approved of the Jewish priests' plans to have Jesus crucified, their conspiracy to taint Him by temptation was not successful.

Notwithstanding the tragedy of His death on the cross, I will have you know that Jesus' Life and Mission were successful. At Pentecost, which was soon after His resurrection and ascension, Jesus poured out His Spirit upon all flesh. At that time He did restrain Lucifer and his agents from the many sinful methods they used to torture and destroy Humans who were so easily taken over by their dark energy. Never again will people become the unwilling hosts of these evil spirits who acted out their devious plans of corruption against Life, Love, and Goodness.

In recent times, Lucifer and his associates have been adjudicated and are restrained from leaving the worlds of their detention. Lucifer did not receive the Divine Mercy and Forgiveness of Lord Jesus simply because he did not accept it when Jesus offered it to him. However, thousands of Angels and other Celestial Personalities, as well as many Material Sons and Daughters, accepted Christ's Mercy and were rehabilitated when Jesus was resurrected 2,000 years ago.

Lucifer stated in his formal reply that he did honor the life and actions of Jesus when He walked the earth as the Son of Man. And because of his close association with Jesus on Earth, Lucifer did give up his evil ways. Lucifer now believes in Me, his Heavenly Father, simply because he believes in the personal integrity of Jesus and knows from his own personal experience that Jesus never lied about Me, even to prevent being tortured to death. Lucifer has offered his repentance for the sinful nature he did embrace. This brilliant Son who strayed so far shall be penalized for his transgressions, but Lucifer will be rehabilitated and given the opportunity to serve his Creator once more, though never again as a ruler in the Heavens.

Many of the crimes against humanity, which were suffered at the hands of these rebellious ones, were due to the nature of My Bestowing free will on all of My Creatures. For it is not through force that I AM worshipped as the God of Endless Mercy and Divine Love. And realize now, My Beloved Ones, that Lucifer and his associates can no longer take over your minds and cause you to suffer or bring brutality upon the meek, for this is no longer permitted. The Lucifer Rebellion is over in Satania and on the Earth, and there shall be no more persecution of Angels or humans any longer.

People are still free to choose evil; however I AM very happy to see that even though the infancy of humanity was so afflicted by the evil purposes of Lucifer, Satan, and the Devil, that so many of you have risen up to follow the Divine

Directives of your Lord Jesus, who is now the acting Planetary Prince of your world.

Yes, humanity has made a remarkable turnaround. There are so many Beautiful Souls who have determined to be good, by cultivating their Divine Attributes and bravely renouncing the evil influences, which have been so prevalent in your societies for so long. There is a vast beauty in the Divine Nature of your Precious Hearts. One day you shall be heralded as Most Supreme Beloved Friends throughout the universes by your associates from other worlds, and in the Angelic Realms on high, because you have overcome so much.

The Second Coming

Dear One,

I would have you know that Jesus is already here with you in Spirit. His Spirit of Truth has pervaded all of you on the Earth, and He truly walks with you in Spirit, as I indwell you also. Look for Him in the reaches of the heart, for that is where He abides. He is here to help you every day and would appreciate it if you would ask Him for His Help and Advice on matters that pertain to your Soul.

My Son is the Spiritual Ruler of this Universe in which you reside. He is even now sitting on the Glorious Throne of Heaven at the Headquarters World of Uversa.* He will be delighted to come to Earth in a form you will recognize, which will be different from any person you have ever seen for He will be in His Glorified Body, which is brilliant with Light. And He will come when the Earth is ready to receive Him, when all Hearts can celebrate His Beloved Return. You should anticipate His Second Coming as you prepare the Gardens of the Lord throughout this Glorious World. You will honor Him by bringing His Personal Logo* to the Earth and displaying it proudly wherever you construct your StarPower* global energy stations.

There will be a great festival of lights when Jesus returns, and you will find His Presence among you, for He will journey around the world to present Himself at the time He returns. You should anticipate His Blessed Coming, for He will truly bring with Him His Angels on High who will also materialize into form and gather around their King. It will be a most blessed event, and you will honor Him and His Legions of Celestial Hosts on every continent around the world. He will visit the temples you shall build in His Honor at the direction of My Emissary, and these will be fitting to receive Him and His Grace, which He shall bestow upon you all at that time. He will be most happy to be received as the Spiritual King of this Blessed World.

It is for you now to prepare a place for Him in your Heart, where He dwells, and in your world, which you may construct into a Heavenly Paradise by your own efforts. This will be the greatest achievement of Humanity, and We all look forward to the great celebration when My Will is done on Earth as It is in Heaven and My Son is elevated to the Throne of Glory where He may reside befittingly, for He does honor and cherish this Blessed World where He walked as a man and brought forth the Divine Ideals of Christhood as He revealed My Nature to Humankind.

So be of good cheer, My Darling One. He has prepared a place for you in Heaven, in the glorious halls of My Mansion Worlds. So prepare a place for Him, to honor Him, as the King of Heaven on Earth.

Christianity in the Golden Age of Light

Dear One,

Do proclaim your Love for and your abiding Faith in the Son of Man. For when Jesus walked the Earth as a man twenty centuries ago, He left a Legacy of Mercy and Love that will live on through the ages to come as the Greatest Example of Living Divinity the world has ever known. Jesus was given the title of Christ because of His Light. Humanity's new beginning is measured from the day that Jesus ascended, for His exemplary life gave rise to the new and enlightened species of humanity who have come forth to live the principles of the Morality he taught, called after his name: Christianity.

My Divine Son came to show humanity an example of how you can be, and now it is up to you to give His Teachings full meaning and verify the True Concept of the Christed One you are becoming with every breath. Hold this Covenant as you would hold a sacred babe within your arms and realize this babe is the Living Christ you are becoming at this time.

You are the Treasure of My Heart. You are the Treasure of the entire Universe. Your Love makes it so, My Darling One. I would have you know that there will come a time, soon to be, when you will be raised up to Shine with the Light of a Thousand Stars. Your Beauty will become so great, and all this will transpire as you pursue Divinity. For you have the Nobility of Perseverance and the Attitude of Trust in your Heavenly Father that ordains your coming of age. It is True that you are My Child and likewise True that you will one day grow up to become a god or goddess of Paradise.

In all you say and do, endeavor to be kind and honor the differences of My Many Diverse Creatures who live here on Earth with you, for I AM within each and every one of them, and My Life is the Life you all live. Cherish this Life and become a Divine One who makes Life a Sacred Treasure and regards it as such, for I AM the Treasure you hold within your loving embrace.

Jesus said, "I AM the Light that lighteth every man who cometh into the world." I AM the Christ you may attain through your diligent endeavors to emulate My Perfection and become all you truly can become. For I AM your Potential and I AM the Living Christ, which is even now becoming part of your splendid personality.

Yes, My Darling One, this is a most auspicious day, and I AM so glad you have taken the time from your many duties and endeavors to proclaim yourself a Child of God, for the Christ Light does surely dwell within you, as it shone within Jesus in those days in Bethlehem so long ago. It would be wise for you to begin, in all you say and do, to hold the Covenant of Christ foremost in authority, for this is the authority you command by your Divine Emergence into Christ-Consciousness.

Don the Divine Raiment, the Garment of Light I bestow upon you now, for this is the Light of Love for all. This is the Light that lighteth every way. This is My Legacy for you. You are My Divine Child, and I AM so pleased with you this day. Please be kind in all you say and do, for I will be here with you and help you to remember your Christhood,

My Blessed One, speak to your friends and neighbors anew. Bless this Earth and bring her to a State of Beauty like unto the original Paradise I planned here so long ago. Delve into the most beautiful thoughts and experiences that you may partake of as your own Beloved Mantel of Glory, for as you are glorified, My Beloved One, you become a Living Christ.

These are the most trying times the world has ever known, yet your brightness is so full of Love that you do charm the Angels who listen for your Laughter and join in along with you as you brighten your days for yourself and others who are graced by your presence. I AM so happy that you have this Divine sense of Love and Appreciation.

My Darling, know this to be true: You shall have this wonderful sense of Beauty follow you all the days of your life and on to the hereafter where We will Laugh together and Sing on High.

Hallelujah!

So do be Charming as you go about your days to every Dear Soul that is Blessed by your presence, and you will indeed impart a Goodness which all desire to receive in the innermost reaches of their Hearts. You do a fine service for Me, bringing forth the Splendid Joy and Friendliness you offer to strangers. Continue this practice, My Precious One, and I shall surely Grace you with all of the Love your Heart can hold.

I AM

A note from the author

I would like to tell you just a little bit about my life, so you can know who is bringing forth God's Words in His Own Name. For most of my life, I thought of myself as separate from God. And although I loved Him very much and honored Him, I did not understand where He was. Even though Jesus said, "The kingdom of God is within you," still, I did not realize it. I thought that God lived high off in His heavenly clouds looking down over me. It did not occur to me that He was here within me all the time.

When I was sixteen years of age, I experienced death. I must have been poisoned, because I became so violently ill that I did not have the strength to stand or walk. My sister carried me up the stairs and laid me in my bed. I wretched and dry heaved until I became so weak I couldn't move at all. The pain and sickness were unbearable. And then, everything went black. I saw a spotlight focused on the back of a man's head. Slowly he turned around and I was horrified to see that it was the Devil, and he was laughing at me.

I prayed for Lord Jesus to help me. Suddenly, it seemed as if I were at the bottom of the ocean with a whirlpool sucking me down. I couldn't breathe. I swam, struggling against the current with all my might. It took every ounce of strength I possessed. As I rose, I noticed that the water got stiller towards the top and easier to ascend. Above me, I could see the surface. I swam on until at last, I broke through where I could breathe.

To my astonishment, I kept ascending right up through the peaking waves. I looked down, and in complete surprise, saw what I had believed to be the ocean was the atmosphere of Earth. I had risen above it into space. I could see the whole world below me. It was infinitely beautiful to behold. I looked towards the sun and it was magnificent, so brilliant! Then I saw, in the far distance, two beautiful Angels shining brighter than the sun. They were flying towards me. A thrill of joy went through me as I thought, "They are going to take me to God." How beautiful they looked. They were the most beautiful beings I had ever seen, and yet, I didn't even have eyes to see. I didn't have a body at all, just a point of consciousness that could behold all the wonder and beauty around me.

When I started out towards them, I heard a Great Voice within me saying, "Wait there. You do not understand how it is." The Voice was kind, compassionate, infinitely loving, neither male nor female, pure, all-powerful, yet gentle... a Voice that seemed to come from the heart of eternity.

As the Angels came closer they spoke, and their words rang all around me and through me. "It is your Father's will," they said, "that you return to Earth. There is something of utmost importance that must be done during your lifetime, something that only you can do." I thought to myself, "Who, me? What could I possibly do that could make a difference?" And then it dawned on me, "Oh, they must have a case of mistaken identity. They have confused me with someone else, someone important."

The Angels said, "Do you want to do your Fathers will?" I felt disappointed, because I really wanted to be with God more than anything. Yet, there was no way to argue with a question like that. "Yes," I thought. "I do want to do my Father's will." And, as I resigned myself to His will, I suddenly sped through the atmosphere until I came to a stop, hovering just above my house.

I had super vision and super hearing! I saw my friend asleep in his bed through the rooftop of his house, three houses away. I could hear his dog breathing. In awe, I began to look around. Then I heard the Angles again; "Do you want to do your Father's will?

As I thought, "Yes," I descended through my rooftop, hovering near the ceiling above my dead body. Surprisingly, I was repulsed by it. Although I had enjoyed my life, I had no desire to go back into that cold lump of flesh. Then, I heard the Angels asking me again, "Do you want to do your Father's will?" And as I thought, "Yes," I suddenly flew into my body. I was stuck, and it felt as if I weighed a thousand pounds, considering a few moments earlier I had the freedom of weightlessness. I was tired, so very tired, but I thanked Jesus because the sickness was gone and I was safe.

What I had been brought back to Earth for, my mission, was to bring God's Words to you now, so you may feel the direct personal experience of His Divine Love. It is God's Will that people everywhere receive the benefit of His Divine Guidance, so everyone can experience the peace, the blessed abundance, and absolute joy of Heaven on Earth now.

I focused on God a lot through my life, and He has spoken to me occasionally, always with miraculous consequences. My life was spared on numerous occasions, from horrific car crashes to attempted murder. By listening to God's Guidance, I have overcome many seeming tragedies and recovered from crippling connective tissue disease. When doctors gave me no hope of recovery from an autoimmune disease that landed me in a wheelchair, I was led by God's Unerring Guidance to a remarkable recovery. I have endured many broken bones, including a broken back, and all these have healed completely. When I was healing, I had more time to focus on improving my spiritual life, so I made God my full-time job.

In 1991 I focused on Him five to seven hours each day for nine months. Each morning I hiked up a remote sea cliff an hour before dawn. There I sat in God-Contemplation* for an hour before sunrise. Every day I felt His Divine Love and experienced ultimate peace. I reached the breathless state and experienced cosmic consciousness. God always opened my eyes the exact moment the sun began to rise, so I could behold His Light. Dolphins gathered by the hundreds in the sea below me.

Motionless, they floated, their dorsal fins rising above the surface of the water. Then, when I rose and stretched forth my hands to bless them, they would all jump at once, spinning with glee. Beyond them, families of great Humpback whales gathered, and closer in to the shore, ancient sea turtles clustered together below me. Above me, giant albatross' circled overhead, while my horse and little dog stood at attention before me. They all lined up for my blessing, for they loved receiving the gift of God's Pure Energy. I spoke aloud, blessing the creatures of the air, the land, and the sea. Then my blessing also reached out to you, flowing all around the world, gracing every person and all life everywhere.

Earlier, in 1981, Jesus had come to me in Spirit. He said, "I want to come through you." Thinking that He wanted to be born into the world again, I got pregnant that very month. I gave birth to a son, whom I called Jesse Kuhio Kalani (which means, God's gracious gift, a prince of Heaven). Jesse is, indeed, heaven sent. He is so filled with nurturing love and helpful wisdom that at Hana grade school, his class made up a special award, to honor him for being the most caring and sharing child in his school. But, ten years later, in 1991, when I was blessing all the world, Jesus came to me again, exactly as He had in the past. Again He said, "I want to come through you." Confused, I said, "I gave birth to Jesse so you could walk the earth again." Then Jesus said with extra emphasis on the last word this time, "I want to come through YOU."

When God asked me to be His emissary, I was worried that I wasn't good enough, or pious enough, or serious enough. I was always kidding around, so I thought that I'd better change my demeanor. Then He told me not to change a thing. He said, "Be light and joyful. Your laughter is especially loved by Me, and the Angels adore it." He said He loved me just the way I was and that when anything needed to be changed in me, He would make the changes.

In 1978, I asked God to take care of my financial needs so that I could work for Him full time, and He has provided for me in many surprising ways. God has also given me the ability to heal others, from migraine headaches to depression. He asked me to write about the miracles He brought into my life during Our Adventures Together, which is the subject of my forthcoming autobiography. Working for God through the years, I have written two screenplays and have compiled manuscripts for fifteen books thus far. Writing was hard for me, for I had to overcome both dyslexia and being an atrocious speller.

When I took the screenplay I had written for God to Hollywood, I met Gene Roddenberry, who offered me the opportunity to have a starring role, as a very spiritual, celibate alien in his first movie, "Star Trek, the Motion Picture." But, following God's Guidance, I turned him down, as well as an opportunity to star in the screenplay I had written. Saying no to these opportunities was the hardest test for me; but God had a greater career planned for me: a life devoted only to Him, far away from the distractions of the fast-paced, worldly, city life, where I could become divine by focusing my attention on God alone. He showed me a vision of a beautiful paradise, a pristine beach where the sun rose from the sea with a hillside pasture for my horse, SunDancer. So I moved to Kauai and after some searching, found the promised land.

In 1996, God asked me to record His Words for the new millennium verbatim. He asked me to bring a little hand held recorder when I came to commune with Him, rather than later trying to remember what I thought I had heard Him say. God also asked me to change my name to I AM. It was challenging, because I felt people would scrutinize me, or think I was crazy, or judge me as being egotistical for claiming I was God. Oh, how I wished He had asked me to build an ark instead... (not that I could have!) But now, I am happy that I did change my name and I know He's happy too, because every time I meet someone in His Name, I AM, the conversation always leads straight to God.

I AM is God, because the Great I AM is alive and conscious in everything, as everything. Every one of us is divinely blessed to be part of God's unfolding miracle of love and life. I feel so reverent to know that I am part of God, that His very Spirit is at the core of my being, that He talks to me, and guides me, and gives me His Divine Love. Now He wants to do that for you too.

People often ask me how I hear God. When I was younger, talking to God was like a one-way telephone conversation. I did all the talking and then hung up with a reverent "Amen." One day, I was inspired to listen. I decided to still my thoughts. It is impossible to think our own thoughts and hear God's Thoughts at the same time, because He will never intrude upon our thoughts. And so, I had to really focus on listening and not let any thoughts come to mind. It was hard at first. Sometimes He would only give me one word and I would have to wait for ten minutes to get the next one. And then, when I got a word wrong, one I thought He was going to say, or a thought came to mind getting in the way, He would stop. Then I would have to go back and see where I had gotten it wrong and begin again. He was very careful not to let me get any words wrong.

At our core, every one of us refers to ourselves as I am, though usually in the context of "I am hungry," or "I am full." God created us in His Image and His Divine Spirit lives in us, as us. When we seek His Inner Guidance and choose to do His Will, we become godly. By contemplating God's Divine Nature and feeling Divine Love, we eventually become divine personalities who identify with God's Holy Spirit, rather than thinking what we have been taught to believe, which is that we are ego based identities, unworthy of and separate from God.

When we experience a divine merger with God's Indwelling Spirit, we are elevated to the joyous throne of Heaven within. There, we celebrate a Divine Marriage of Sacred Spirit, and become Temples of the Most High Living God!

I have aligned my will with His Will, and my soul is filled with His Holy Spirit. I realize that I AM God's Living Temple. I have invited Him to speak up whenever He likes. Now, He wants to speak through me, to everyone on Earth.

At the burning bush, when God asked Moses to free His enslaved people, Moses asked God, "Who shall I say has sent me?" God replied, "I AM." Moses didn't understand, so God repeated, "I AM that I AM." But God could not get through the rigid constructs of Moses' ingrained beliefs. Moses could only conceive of God as Jehovah: angry, jealous, and wrathful. He was, to Moses, the God of the fiery volcano, who vented while Moses delivered the Ten Commandments to the Hebrews. That is the reason there are so many conflicting views of God's nature within Biblical scriptures. Jesus knew Moses' interpretation of God's nature was incorrect, so He taught that the One True God, whose name is I AM, is our loving Heavenly Father who resides in the Heaven within our hearts. Jesus said, "The Kingdom of God is within you."

Jesus realized God's presence within Himself and received God's Divine Love and Guidance directly. He spoke God's thoughts, proclaiming, "I AM the light of the world." He tried to explain to people, saying, "These things I tell you, I say not of myself. It is the Father within me that doeth the works." But, unless people have had a firsthand experience of God within themselves, it is a very hard concept to understand, especially when they have been taught to believe that God is a mighty fearful Deity that lives somewhere else. Believing it was heresy and blasphemy to profess union with God, many people thought Jesus was egotistically speaking about himself, and so, misunderstood His teachings and condemned Him. Jesus said that we are all sons and daughters of God. Yet after His death, people who didn't really understand what Jesus was trying to say wrote the Bible. Consequently, they referred to "God's chosen people" as being the Hebrews exclusively. In fact, all people are God's people and for those who are enslaved, God always does His best to inspire someone to set them free.

God wants each and every one of us to have an intimate love-relationship with Him. It is possible for you also to merge with Him and develop your power to heal yourself and others. Jesus said, "These things and greater things shall ye do also." Let us prove Him right by creating Heaven on Earth now in this new millennium, for "God's Kingdom will come, when His Will is done, on Earth as it is in Heaven."

Testimonial by God's Emissary's Son

My mother, I AM, is GOD's emissary and interpreter. I have always loved my mother; she has never hurt me in any way. She has always been there for me. I believe in her. The ascension of light and goodness has always been her goal. Whether she was planting trees, writing screenplays or working on *Gods Words*, she always had time for me. For that reason I shall love her forever. The dawn of a new era approaches. Great changes will occur. The human race can only pray for the best, and the best is what will come.

The age of light is here.

Jesse Best

age 16

Be an Earth Angel and join God's A-Team of Volunteers who create Heaven on Earth.

You can participate in Paradise reconstruction and in the enlightenment of humanity. If you have time, a talent, or resources you would like to contribute, please let us know how you can help.

Projects are currently underway for:

Publishing God's ongoing transcripts. Calling all Angels to help finance the publishing of God's Words in order to make mass distribution and donations of books, audio tapes, and CD-ROMs possible.

Angel Art representing all nationalities sought to decorate God's Words.

Linguists sought to help translate God's Words into every language.

Centers are required worldwide to organize God's A-Team for the global reconstruction of Paradise. God's Children of all faiths are welcome. Perhaps your church, mosque, synagogue, temple, club, or organization would like to join this multi-denominational movement to create Heaven on Earth.

TV and radio shows and advertisements can spread the good word. Publicity in magazines, newspapers, and on the internet is essential.

www.IAMLOVE.TV - God's TV ministry convenes in cyberspace. Please join us and share your practical ideas for creating Heaven on Earth, for you and those around you.

One tree can make a difference for 200 years. Earth Angels like you can start fruit or nut trees that will help end world hunger. To find out about these projects and more log on to:

www.IAMLOVE.TV

I AM Love

God's Word Definitions

I AM Love

* rule – the body of regulations prescribed by the founder of a religious order for governing the conduct of its members
* court – God's governing body, Ancients of Days in the superuniverses and Paradise Creator Sons in the local universes
* predicated – based on
* Emergence – to come into existence

My Holy Nature

* inanimate – lifeless, such as material things, inorganic matter and unorganized matter
* retribution – judgment and punishment for sins
* base – lowly, inferior in quality or value
* tyranny – absolute power exercised unjustly or cruelly

My True Nature

* Yahweh - also Yahveh, Jahveh, Jahweh, or Jehovah
    A Hebrew name for God assumed by modern scholars to be a rendering of the pronunciation of the Tetragrammaton
* abominable - unequivocally detestable, loathsome

Your Perfect Destiny

* architectural worlds - are material worlds though not evolutionary in nature. They are created by Celestial Personalities who are Master Architects.
* Grand Universe - comprised of the Seven Super Universes, the Divine Master Universe and the Central Isle of Paradise
* aggregations - amassments, accumulations
* Morontia - The transitory experience between material and Spiritual. Human beings are resurrected in Morontia bodies, the same type of form that Jesus appeared to His disciples in after He was resurrected.
* incumbent - holding the office of divine beneficiary, coheir
* three brained - some otherworldly humans have a triune intellect; three main interrelated trio-spheres, being right, left, and fore-brained

The Holy Family of Heaven

* triune – three in one, constituting a trinity in unity as the Godhead
* cohesion – the intermolecular attraction by which the elements of a body are held together
* facilitating – to make easy or easier
* visit – to make itself known

Truth

* embellishment – adding fictitious or ornamental details that embellish the true story, making it seem more interesting or important.

My Divine Son

* exemplify – To illustrate by example
* willfully – said or done on purpose, deliberate, voluntary
* Nebadon – The Universe of Nebadon is the Heavenly Kingdom of Jesus Christ, which is comprised of ten thousand galaxies, including approximately 10 million inhabitable worlds in prospect, over three million of which are now populated.
* alleviate – relieve

* Epitome of Righteousness – the representative example of Right, Goodness, and Virtue
* heinous – hateful
* Sanhedrin – the highest judicial and ecclesiastical council of the ancient Jewish nation, comprised of from 70 to 72 members
* Portrayal – Jesus' dramatic representation of divinity in flesh
* formidable – awesome, influential
* circumventing – to go around; bypass
* paradigm – the standard, an example that serves as pattern or model
* superstition – a belief or practice resulting from ignorance
* occult – matters pertaining to supernatural powers

The Myth of Armageddon

* figurative – based on or making figures of speech; symbolic
* end of days – interpretation of the Revelations prophesy that the world would end (at the end of the past millennium) and the good people would be raptured– (taken off the earth) before Armageddon.
* imminence – something about to occur
* edifying – establishing beliefs by instruction in a religious way

My Divine Self

* Personage – God's divine image, the Almighty I AM
* gay – bright, witty, lively, pleasant, light-minded, dashing, flamboyant, showy, brave, gallant, jaunty, sporty, merry and wise

Treasure of the Heart

* penchant – predisposition, a unique special talent for expressing your feelings.

Your Heavenly Mother

* committing – to make known the views of (oneself) on an issue
* indwell – A Divine inner Spirit dwells within you

The Mission of Jesus

* Universal Sovereign – the all powerful monarchical ruler of an entire universe who exercises supreme authority and control
* Nebadon – the Universal name of our Universe
* kinship – family

Divine Life Currents

* paramount – imperative, high priority, overruling
* emancipated – freed, liberated, delivered, saved or discharged
* primordial energies of space – space potency, antimatter, the Universe Force Charge of space
* Emergent Life: completely new types of organisms and characteristics Suddenly appear at certain stages of the evolutionary process, due to the Creator's permeation of the Divine Life Currents with heightened Life Force, which results in the beneficial rearrangement of preexisting elements
* nebula – the ancestors of the Universes
* Divinely Endowed – to be blessed and empowered with

The Truth of Creation

* mythologies – a body of myths belonging to a people, addressing their origin, history, deities, ancestors, and heroes
* surmise – presume, suspect
* erroneous – containing or derived from error or mistake
* hypothesized – a theory, an assumption based on limited knowledge

* fulgurant - flashing like lightning; brilliant
* Adamic Bestowal - the gift-mission of Adam and Eve, biologic uplifters of humanity
* admixture - superior genetic strands of DNA were a product of mixing human and Adamic blood through inter-racial reproduction
* DNA - cell nuclei that forms the molecular basis of heredity
* precepts - religious teachings
* Urantia Book - Copyright 1955, The Urantia Foundation
* Urantia - the universal name of planet Earth, pronounced: u-ron-T-a (roll the r slightly)

Adam and Eve

* DNA - a nucleic acid that carries the hereditary information in the cell and is capable of self-replication and synthesis of RNA. The sequence of nucleotides determines individual heredity characteristics.
* Jerusem is the System Capital world of Satania, a sparcly populated system with currently 619 inhabited worlds, including Earth. Many more planets will eventually be habitable in over 500 solar systems.
* doning - being a donor; donating

The Lucifer Rebellion

✳ Nebadon - The Universe of Nebadon is the Heavenly Kingdom of Jesus Christ (whose Universal title is Michael of Nebadon). Nebadon is comprised of ten thousand galaxies including approximately 10 million inhabitable worlds in prospect, over three million of which are now inhabited.

The Second Coming

✳ Uversa - capitol of this Universe, Nebadon.
✳ logo - identifying statement or symbol
✳ StarPower - A global solar energy invention that will supply fresh pure water, vegetarian protein and safe clean electrical energy, the basic necessities of life for everyone on the planet.

In this 21st Century update, GOD's Divine Plan to create **Heaven on Earth now** is revealed for all humanity. Feel a direct personal experience of GOD's Divine Love as you read these Holy Books for All the Ages.

Profits from the sales of these books will help create Heaven on Earth.

✠
Enjoy
Beautifully
Illustrated, Inspiring
Messages in full color
& b&w Books, Audio Cassettes,
Videos, e-books, and on CD Rom.

Join the Movement to Create
Heaven on Earth
IAMLOVE.TV

Heaven on Earth
Order Form

Phone orders Toll Free: 1-800-795-3069
E-mail: Godswords@IAMLOVE.TV
Postal orders: Heaven on Earth
P.O. Box 398
Hanalei, Hawaii 96714

Rich with Angelic art, each book contains 200+ pages of beautifully illustrated, inspiring messages from Heaven. Quality paperbacks, signed by author...$19.95 each. Beautiful hard cover, full color, limited, signed, collectors edition ... $99.95 each.

Please send me the following books shown on the other side:
_____
_____

☐   Please send God's Heaven on Earth newsletter to me **FREE.**
☐   I have enclosed a question for God or my prayer request.

Company name:_____
Name:_____
Address:_____
City, state, zip:_____
Telephone: (_____)_____ e-mail:_____

US Shipping; $4.00 for the first book and $2.00 each additional book.
International Shipping: $8 for the first book and $4 for each additional book.
Please make check made payable to: Heaven on Earth
Credit cards: ☐ VISA   ☐ MC
Card Number:_____
Name on card:_____ Exp. date:_____/____

"This book cured my depression. God's Words really make me feel good inside. Thank you, I AM, for writing this miracle. I recommend it to everyone!"
---Crystal Horne, Kapaa, Hawaii

"I can feel the wondrous experience of GOD's Almighty Love coursing through His Words." ---Jim Shidler, carpenter, Kalaheo, Kauai

"God's Words for a new Millennium of Heaven on Earth gave me a divine connection to Heaven within. Reading this book made me a better person."
---Charles Lester, merchant, Kapaa, Hawaii

"IT IS SIMPLY THE GREATEST BOOK THAT HAS EVER BEEN WRITTEN!"
--- David Allison, sculptor and artist, Kilauea, Hawaii

"Written to those who live in this millennium, GOD's Words of love and guidance speak to today's needs and situations. If you have any doubt as to their authenticity, just read. God's Words by I AM will speak to your heart like no other.".---Dave Ruskjer, computer software specialist and choir director, Poipu Beach, Hawaii

"By divine intervention, God is speaking to us now. Let us listen! This book gives us our promise of tomorrow. If we wait 'till tomorrow to save the garden, it will be too late. If we implement God's plan now, then we will have a tomorrow." ---Debra Turner, US Army and Deputy Sheriff, Salem, Oregon, retired

"If people everywhere would just live this truth for one moment, the whole world would be changed for the better forever." ---Raynella Solandra, DVM

"Highly inspirational and thought provoking. I AM is an original visionary of the first order. She is indeed, a jewel in the crown of life."---Ronald Dixon, Princeville, HI

"REVOLUTIONARY! God's Words by I AM are deeply impactfull for the new millennium."
--- Dr. Ann West, "Truth from the Source" radio talk show host, KKCR Hanalei

The author first began writing for God in 1979. Over the years, her connection, and her communication skills with GOD increased, and in 1991, on a secluded bay in Kauai, during her sunrise meditations, GOD began speaking to her directly, asking her to record His messages for humanity verbatim. Over the years, the author has brought forth hundreds of GOD's divine essays, which she has compiled into beautifully illustrated, heavenly books, rich with angelic art. These sacred volumes will bless this New Millennium with hope as they reveal God's divine plan for Heaven on Earth now. Feel a direct personal experience of GOD's Divine Love as you read these Holy Books for all the ages.

www.ingramcontent.com/pod-product-compliance
Lightning Source LLC
Chambersburg PA
CBHW081834170426
43199CB00017B/2730